Santa Clara County Free Library

REFERENCE

CALIFORNIA QUAKE

CALIFORNIA QUAKE

Larry L. Meyer

SHERBOURNE PRESS
Nashville, Tennessee

Library of Congress Cataloging in Publication Data:
Meyer, Larry L   1933-

  California quake.

  Includes index.
  1. Earthquakes—California.   2. Earthquake prediction.
  3. Disaster relief—California.
  I. Title.
  QE535.2.U6M47   551.2′2′09794   76-44275
  ISBN 0-8202-0134-0

For Eric, Kurt, and Karl

CONTENTS

FOREWORD

Senator Alan Cranston

A major earthquake in our nation today would be more devastating than anything we have ever known. Our country is densely populated and millions of Americans are concentrated in large and vulnerable cities, where a quake would not only bring terrible loss of life and property but deal a serious blow to our national economy and psyche.

It has been estimated that more human beings died in 1976 in earthquakes than in any year since the sixteenth century—since 1556, actually, when the Shensi Province quake in China killed 820,000. The United States was spared in 1976 from the tragedies that befell China, Italy, Guatemala and the Philippines. But there's no reason to believe we will be spared indefinitely. Two-thirds of our citizens, residing in thirty-nine states, live in potentially dangerous earthquake areas. California and Alaska top the list, but seismic risks are high in such widely separated states as Utah, Massachusetts, South Carolina, Kentucky, Missouri and Montana, to name only a few.

With these grim realities there is also now hope from scientists who have recently made great advances in understanding the causes of earthquakes. There is well-founded hope that with a well-directed, well-funded national research program, we will have the capacity within the next ten years to know at least where and when earthquakes will strike.

My own commitment to earthquake prediction as a national goal began about five years ago, and then as a chance outgrowth of another interest of mine: I'd long been a backer of arms limitations and a nuclear test ban treaty, but like many other people, wondered: how could one side know if the other were abiding by an agreement? Could, for example, detection devices discriminate between a natural earthquake and a nuclear explosion? An expert with the Department of Defense assured me that the means were being developed to do just that. He said earthquakes give advance warnings, bomb detonations do not. I immediately began quizzing him as to whether these "advance warnings" meant earthquakes could be predicted. His answer, and the answer I received from other experts, was: Yes, provided sufficient funds and manpower were invested in research to expand research on earthquake prediction and ways to reduce their hazards. Though we are still without a comprehensive research program, I feel encouraged by recent developments. My bill was overwhelmingly passed by the Senate last year. Its companion in the House of Representatives was defeated only on a procedural motion. Meanwhile, the Chinese, Russians and Japanese continue their own considerable efforts at earthquake prediction, and our awareness of what remedies are possible continues to grow.

California, of course, is the most likely candidate for our next big earthquake. In the past Californians have experienced the worst of them, and they may have become fatalistic. Understandably not wanting to leave California, they've tended to put the subject out of mind. But they are becoming aware that, given advance warning, there are a number of things they can do to lessen earthquake damage: turn off gas and electricity to prevent fires, lower water levels behind dams to prevent flood, evacuate buildings especially susceptible to collapse, put into action emergency communications and medical, water, and food distribution systems.

It is now a race against time: will the U.S. be ready for the next major earthquake, whether it strikes California or any of the other forty-nine states?

Mr. Meyer's book is a most readable account of where we stand in that race, explaining in layman's language the major breakthroughs in geophysics in the past few years and how Californians are facing up to the prospect of another big tremor. As a bonus, it also makes for engaging reading in the history of our most populous and prosperous state.

SENATOR ALAN CRANSTON

INTRODUCTION

Earthquakes do more than shake the earth. When felt by man (the wise one who can remember the past and fret about the future) they shake his deeply held assumption that he belongs on this swirling sphere. Terra firma suddenly proves less than firm, and he is confronted with a terror qualitatively different from others of his own or even nature's making.

Charles Darwin left us with perhaps the best brief description of what it is like to survive a major tremor. He was in Chile at the time, put in at the port of Valdivia during his celebrated voyage aboard the *Beagle,* when a severe shake awakened him on that long ago morning in the 1830s.

"A bad earthquake at once destroys our oldest associations," he wrote in his *Journal of Research.* "The earth, the very emblem of solidity, has moved beneath our feet like a fluid;—one second of time has created in the mind a strange idea of insecurity which hours of reflection would not have produced."

Few who have experienced a major earthquake would quarrel with the great naturalist. To have Mother Earth suddenly, without warning, turn to undulating jelly beneath one's feet is to feel the ultimate betrayal, know the ultimate rejection.

Among natural catastrophes, earthquakes rank as the greatest killers. One scientific estimate puts the human lives lost at 75 million since man first appeared on this shuddering planet. The reasons why are not hard to come by. Storms and floods and such are presaged by signs that can be measured, or at least observed. Earthquakes just happen, all at once, unannounced and unexpected; and the destructive energy released by a massive shift within the earth's crust makes the power of the largest thermonuclear bomb yet detonated seem trifling by comparison.

1

CALIFORNIA QUAKE

There is a special irony in the hazards posed by earthquakes. Man is most vulnerable to them in the centers of his civilization, in his cities, where nature has been largely banished and where he would like to feel secure. Here the most visible accomplishments of his industry can, in less than a minute, come crashing lethally down on his brain, that miraculous organ that allowed him to build them in the first place.

The United States has not suffered nearly as much from quakes as other countries. To date, fewer than 1,200 lives have been taken by earth tremors. But then the United States is a young nation, and the increasingly vertical concentration of its citizens in increasingly vertical cities is more recent still. Meaning that the worst is before us, not behind us. Meaning that we'll be paying our national dues at some future time.

Many Americans live on land that is reasonably anchored, and are strangers to the national disasters that have befallen China, Chile, or Japan. Yet the nation has its own seismically active regions, most notably California, now the most populous and prosperous of the fifty united states. Alaska, Washington and Montana also have been severely shaken in the last three decades. But, in historic times, California has experienced more devastating tremors than all the other forty-nine states.

Author Carey McWilliams has aptly called California "the Great Exception." That it is—or has become, in its climate, culture, exportation of life-styles, and the restless experimentation and sunstruck hedonism of its people. But if Californians are unpredictable, the same is true of the ground they stand on. The state's 158,690 square miles of staggering geographical variety are fractured dominantly (but not exclusively) by the notorious San Andreas Fault, a northwest-southeast-running rift that separates what, geologically speaking, are really two Californias. The third of the land southwest of the fault is slowly moving, relatively speaking, by creep and by jerk, in a northwesterly direction. The rest of the state is shoving its way west, in the direction of continuing confrontation. And that means earthquakes. At the rate the two segments are moving, some eight million years from now Los Angeles will be directly west of San Francisco—a fact that will doubtlessly please Angelenos, who have traditionally enjoyed visiting "the City" for its good food and the good life; as for San Franciscans, given their long-standing airs, the prospect of such a neighbor will certainly cause shudders unrelated to any local buckling of the earth.

A more immediate worry, for both Angelenos and San Franciscans, not to mention those Golden Staters living between them, are all those necessary bumps and grinds that will attend any such long-term geographical displacement. There is general agreement that California is overdue for a giant earthquake. The last great thrust along the San Andreas Fault was in 1906, when San Francisco was reduced to flaming rubble, and before that the Los Angeles section lurched violently northward in 1857, wrenching a largely unpopulated landscape.

Those who predict a calamitous quake for California are not limited to cranks and soothsayers. Scientists have lately warned of shocks to come, both on the basis of the historical record and some dramatic new breakthroughs in the field of seismology. An ominous swelling in the earth of the Mojave Desert, known in California as the Palmdale Bulge, portends ill for the Los Angeles area. But major adjustments in the California crust are also expected elsewhere; if not tomorrow, then next month. If not next month, then next year, or the next decade. They will come.

To say that Californians are sitting on a powder keg is to resort to an inadequate metaphor. What they're sitting on, and building their homes and schools and businesses on, is a locked and straining earth with a potential destructive force of a whole arsenal of fusion bombs. And when one of the big ones does "go off" near a major population center, the predictions are of an unprecedented natural disaster, the property loss measured in the tens of billions of dollars, the toll in lives counted in the tens of thousands.

Such figures are chilling indeed. Yet most Californians seem to go blithely on, living their lives and enjoying themselves, as though earthquakes were only made in Hollywood. Senator Alan Cranston, the concerned author of legislation meant to fund seismic research and earthquake prediction, believes Californians are fatalistic when it comes to earthquakes. One might add that they are also largely ignorant of them—at least those of the magnitude that rocked the state in the last century and are expected to do so again. Some residents of course remember all too well the Long Beach tremor of 1933, the Bakersfield jolt of 1952, the San Fernando temblor of 1971. But those were just moderate-size quakes, mere terrestrial shrugs when compared to the giant spasms—those registering eight-plus magnitude on the Richter Scale—that the land is heir to.

For every Californian of today who has had his home quiver and his cupboards emptied of dishes, there's another who has never felt an earthquake. He or she may live in a temporarily quiet region. Or be one of those countless recent arrivals to the Golden State. That in part may account for the continued buying of homes built right on top of known fault lines; for the continued occupancy of structures that are known to be unsafe; for the real estate interests which condone public ignorance of the danger; for government officials, including the present governor, who pinch dollars that might at least mitigate the tragic consequences of the next big quake. Where fatalism ends and foolishness begins is a very fine line indeed. It's almost as though today's Californians, most of whom are dislocated sons and daughters of Northern Europe recently arrived in the Promised Land, know deep down that all the fun they've had has to be paid for, *somehow!*

Some Americans living outside the Golden State have a jaundiced view of California. They know it as a fount of novelty and lunacy, the devil's own playground. And if the advertised catastrophe does strike California, there are historical precedents. After all, Sodom and Gomorrah paid for their sins; the pirates' den of Port Royal got its comedownance.

However uncharitable such sentiments may or may not be, they are certainly shortsighted. A disastrous earthquake in California would bring grief far beyond its borders. Stricken, the agricultural and industrial giant would visit economic dislocations across the nation, and the inevitable grand-scale federal relief measures would bite into everyone's tax dollars.

Another reason why non-Californians should curb any desire to gloat is that earthquakes can, and do, occur most everywhere. In 1811-12, a series of massive tremors, centered around New Madrid, Missouri, rattled the North American continent from Canada to the Atlantic seaboard to the Gulf of Mexico, and are considered the top shocks to have rocked North America in historic times. In 1886 a killer quake struck Charleston, South Carolina. Before then and since, New England has experienced unsteady periods. Upstate New York trembles regularly, and lives have been lost in the unstable Rocky Mountain states. The message that science has only recently unscrambled is that the earth is dynamic, not static, endlessly building and destroying and reforming its surface features. We, it would seem, are merely along for the ride. And no human being, living anywhere on the surface of the restless globe, is immune to having home come tumbling down on self and loved ones.

So much for spreading the bad news around. While earthquakes can strike anywhere, in Minnesota or Texas or California, the laws of probability return the focus of this book to the Golden State, where quakes have periodically interrupted the good life in the past, and where all signs point to one or more big shakes in the near future. After Los Angeles, San Francisco, neighbor to the notorious San Andreas Fault, is widely supposed to be the next most likely target for a major shock, though a tremor along any of California's many other active faults would be no surprise to seismologists.

In 1976 jittery Southern Californians survived two scares. One doomsday forecast for December by a pseudoscientist (who nevertheless gained an astonishing amount of television exposure) came and went without event. Another earthquake figured in the "testing of a scientific hypothesis"—widely interpreted as a prediction by the news media—before it was withdrawn last fall by a respected Caltech seismologist. Southern Californians greeted the two false alarms with cheers, which may be premature to say the least. Serious students of the earth know that, far from getting any new lease on stable ground, the day of reckoning for Southlanders has been merely postponed.

To some respected earth-watchers, including Professor Don Anderson of Caltech, the year 1976 heralded a reawakening of the earth in the seismic sense. A decades-long lull was broken with savage rips that claimed 700,000 lives in headline disasters originating from Guatemala, Italy, the Philippines, China, Turkey and Iran. California is no less quake-prone than those faraway places, and Atlas can be expected to shrug again under the Golden State one of these days, ready or not.

Here, then, is a summary look at California's bigger quakes of the past, a discussion of remarkable recent advances in understanding the cause of earthquakes, and words of hope that the most terrifying on earth's cataclysms may soon be predictable— perhaps, one day, even controllable.

1

THE CHURCH WRECKERS

California owes its very name to impressionable Spaniards who didn't skimp on their escape reading. A medieval chivalric romance written by Garcí Ordoñez de Montalvo, *Las Sergas de Esplandían,* first described a mythical, remote island inhabited by fierce, man-killing black Amazons, and ruled over by their warrior queen Calafía. Gold and silver abounded there, as did griffins and sundry natural wonders.

Conquistadors arriving in the New World brought with them that equivalent of today's paperback, and over the post-Renaissance years the mellifluous name became attached to a mysterious land northwest of the Valley of Mexico. It wasn't easily reached, this California, because the winds were not kind to sailing ships. But it possessed an incontestable magic for romantics everywhere, a place where dreams and desires met.

Sailor Juan Rodríquez Cabrillo reached that distant northern shore in the year 1542. And though the skipper was to die there, his crew brought back to Mexico good news of a happy and fertile coast of much promise. This appraisal was confirmed by the voyages of Sebastian Vizcaíno (1602-3) and a few others, but the Mexico-based administrators of New Spain didn't go rushing out after all that alleged gold and silver and good times. There were more pressing matters to attend to closer to home. And the far land languished in Spanish imaginations and waxed more romantic in a reputation rooted mostly in lies and legend.

Fear finally got Spain off its Bourbon throne in the 1760s and cast it as the dog in the manger. The Russians were said to be invading that gilded coast, and brash Britons who nearly owned the seas were said to be closing in on the Spanish dreamscape. What the spirit of adventure failed to do, the realities of *geopolitik* got done in a hurry. In 1769 Spain decided to take legal possession of what was its own—by all recognized rights of discovery. Spaniards came by land and they came by sea; Captain Gaspar de Portolá and Father Junípero Serra hoofing it overland up the spare backbone of Baja California, and the scurvied survivors of two ships from San Blas rendezvousing with them at what is today San Diego.

It has been reported that among the first things Father Serra learned from the aborigines in the summer of 1769 was that the locals had recently witnessed both a solar eclipse and a traumatic earthquake—the latter, according to the Indians, caused "by the giant who moves in the earth." The sophisticated Europeans' knowledge of astronomy made a fable of any eclipse. As for the earthquake, future events would make that claim far more credible.

Father Serra stayed with the sick in San Diego, while Gaspar de Portolá, the appointed governor of the Californias, a good soldier who followed orders, departed with thirty-five soldiers, twenty-four retainers, and two priests. His superiors had instructed him to locate the Bay of Monterey, which Vizcaíno had praised as a fine natural harbor; to locate it, the march had to be north into unknown territory.

At first the lands the Spaniards traversed seemed to match their billing. The Indians the column of Hispanic horsemen met proved friendly, the pasturage was plentiful, and all was going well. Then, at one o'clock in the afternoon of July 28, 1769, as the party was camped on the banks of a river not far from the Anaheim of today, the very earth leaped beneath their feet—for about "half as long as an Ave Maria," according to Father Juan Crespí, a diarist for the historic adventure. A native shaman visiting the newcomers was as panicked as they, and immediately began entreating the heavens for an end to it. His prayers went unanswered. Ten minutes later another shock bounced them all, to be followed by two more sharp tremors that seemed to come on the hour.

The awed Spaniards called their river the *Rio Jesús de los Temblores,* though it would later be known by a gentler name, the Santa Ana. The Portolá party packed up the next afternoon and headed towards the north and their accidental discovery of San Francisco Bay, but worrisome days of aftershocks were to dog them all the way to the Los Angeles River.

Later geologists have surmised from the expedition's reports that the quake of July, 1769 was a major one, though of course there is no way to assign it a magnitude number. Certainly it must have rattled the Spaniards' nerves and given rise to second thoughts about this land of their dreams, which had trembled beneath their feet within the first few months they occupied it. Yet they stayed on.

Gold and silver were cached in California as the Spaniards believed, but they never found any in the fifty-odd years they had legal title to it. There were also "natural wonders," more demonstrably evident in earthquakes that intermittently rumbled under the sandaled feet of the padres. In one of those unusual instances where politicians take a back seat to prelates, California became a bucolic backwater of the empire, where the Catholic clergy reaped a harvest in heathen souls and the Spanish crown picked up the tab.

Modern Californians love their old Spanish missions. The oldest oldtimer and rawest, rootless newcomer alike have been known to get moist in the eye when they take out-of-state relatives to visit any of the twenty-one missions. They are beautiful; seem to belong on the land as later and new structures do not; relics of a more peaceful time.

Not every choked admirer of mission churches realizes that all those heaps of masonry—as beautiful and architecturally distinctive as they may be—are not the original articles. They are at best restorations. Or restorations of reconstructions. Or reconstructions of restorations of damaged original constructions. And so on. The truth is that those picture postcard edifices were not meant for California's shifting turf, as the Spaniards learned in their time.

The padres and their subject Indian neophytes learned that lesson piecemeal, a quiver at a time. At Mission San Juan Bautista, the fathers were rousted from their beds on October 11, 1800. Mission San Diego de Alcalá was slightly damaged by the tremor of May 25, 1803. Church walls cracked at Santa Barbara on March 24, 1806. Mission Dolores in San Francisco took eighteen shocks in June and July of 1808; the church adobe was a shambles. But all were mere overtures to dreadful things to come.

The year 1812 saw the infant United States going to war with Great Britain a second time to redeem its hard-won independence. On the distant neglected coast across the continent, all was peaceful, as Spanish priests continued to bring civilization to the heathen by way of instruction in the True Faith, the planting of increasingly productive mission fields, and enlarging the herds through animal husbandry. A calm prevailed for the first eleven months of the year, as if an approving God were coddling the missionaries. Then, as always without warning, was ushered in what the Spaniards were to call *"El Año de los Temblores"*—the Year of the Earthquakes.

December 8 fell on a Sunday that dawned clear and warm and still, without even the normal sea breeze that brushed the white walls of Mission San Juan Capistrano. The bells were rung, summoning the faithful to Mass in the recently completed cruciform church, later acknowledged to be the finest architectural achievement of Spain in California.

The service was nearing its end. Some fifty Indian converts prayed in the 90 by 180 foot church, beneath the thick arched roof that was the pride of master mason Isodoro Aguilar. Suddenly, accompanied by a rushing sound, the earth beneath them seemed to rise vertically and rotate horizontally. The massive stones of the dome vibrated, then came plummeting down in a scream of ruptured mortar. It was the luck of the priest at the altar to escape death, along with a handful of Indians in the congregation. But crushed and buried beneath the rubble were some forty worshippers who had been in the wrong place at the right time. Over the next days their bodies would be dug out and given a decent, Christian burial.

There is no way of knowing the magnitude of that quake either; that it was great there can be no doubt. It was felt from San Diego to Santa Barbara. At Mission San Gabriel, more than fifty miles from San Juan Capistrano, the main altar spilled its burden of statues, and the church belltower toppled onto clerical residences. Thankfully, no lives had been lost at San Gabriel, but a new beam-buttressed roof had to be put over the damaged house of worship.

December 8 was soon followed by December 21, and the earth struck again—this time north of the previous grief, at Santa Barbara, where there was a presidio and a mission, and in surrounding areas where there were only missions. Father Gil y Taboada and Marcos Amestoy at Santa Barbara reported that the local church had been battered beyond repair, and several mission buildings were totally destroyed. Presidio Commandante José Argüello was also in a quandary: his stronghold was in ruins, yet the local Spaniards and Indians came to huddle with his soldiers for protection against an enemy he couldn't fight. Worse, the earth wouldn't stop trembling, and continued its anxious movements through the spring of 1813, terrifying one and all and opening in the ground several "sulphur-spewing volcanoes" (probably steam from underground hot water cells forced up under pressure; in a number of California quakes subterranean water has gushed like fountains and created local surface craters of upblown sand).

Spaniards soon learned to their sorrow that the devastation was not localized. At distant San Fernando the church was damaged. At San Buenaventura (Ventura) the mission was fractured and appeared to be sinking into the treacherous earth. Mission Santa Inéz, near today's Danish community of Solvang, had to be rebuilt. Finally, in the peaceful valley where present-day Lompoc basks in the sun, Mission La Purísima Concepción had many of its church buildings and a hundred Indian adobes destroyed. Mission records make no mention of casualties. But according to Walker A. Tompkins, a Santa Barbara historian, a contractor excavating in Lompoc in 1960 unearthed several skeletons buried beneath the fragments of red tiled roofs, which were in turn buried under silt that had washed down on top of the original mission site.

For months, both Spaniards and Indians in the Santa Barbara region abandoned the plaster monuments of New Spain's occupation in favor of reed huts, and births and burials in the wild, where at least walls didn't come tumbling down. It was almost as though God were displeased with the work undertaken on his behalf.

A *tsunami,* or seismic sea wave, was also said to have struck Santa Barbara at the time of the 1812 earthquake. The ocean receded, as it sometimes does when the earth squirms, temporarily exposing its rarely seen bed. Then, in the best tradition of cinema "tidal waves," it came crashing back against the land in a high fury.

One tale tells of a Yankee smuggler who was unloading his ship of forbidden cargo at the time of the *tsunami.* Captain George Washington Ayres had brought his ship *Mercury* all the way from Boston to harvest prized otter skins from the California coast. He also brought a liking for the local brandy; and at his anchorage of six fathoms off Refugio Beach, he had just taken aboard a supply of the fiery elixir, obtained from Don Vicente Ortega in illegal trade. Suddenly a towering wall of water rose and came thundering in. It lifted the *Mercury* like a cork and gave it a roller-coaster ride right up a canyon toward Don Ortega's rancho.

"Our ship," Captain Ayres put down in his log, "was then swept back to deep water by the receding waters of that mighty wave, none the worse for our voyage up a stream which an hour before would not have been too deep for a man to wade across."

The same tale claims that, thus delivered, Ayres hied himself off to Old Mexico—to Guadalajara to be precise—where he spent the rest of his life repenting in comfort. If true, it is the first but hardly the last instance of a gringo felon enjoying his ill-gotten gains south of the present-day border.

The "year of earthquakes" did subside, and the industrious Spaniards did rebuild what nature had razed. All the same, their days under the California sun were numbered. In 1822, Mexico declared its independence from its Old World overlords, not failing to claim the golden land of dreams and promise, California, as its own. That claim would be honored for not quite a quarter-century. Those who would displace the Mexicans rather gracelessly called themselves "Americans" and invoked "Manifest Destiny" to justify what they were about. Rushing westward, no power on earth could stop them.

Nor would the earth at land's end ever sit still for them.

2

THE GRINGO'S WELCOME

The Los Angeles of the 1850s was a scruffy little cow town in the business of selling beef to miners in northern California, where the real action was. The War with Mexico had only recently been concluded, and though the more respectable "Californios" and "Anglos" managed to live together in a strained harmony, the less exalted of the two races mixed it up often, with each other when the opportunity presented itself, among themselves when it did not.

Gamblers had the run of the dusty town. Horsethieves were as pesky as horseflies, and some said as numerous. Street knifings and shootings relieved the small town tedium almost daily. Given all this mischief, it is not surprising that lynchings ranked high on the list of favored public entertainments—second only to a lively fandango, those impromptu fiestas benefiting from their comparative rarity.

What Los Angeles needed, its decent citizens were agreed, was a heavy dose of good old law and order, an "authority" with some muscle behind it, a federal presence in their neglected corner of the vast, raw, new Golden State. Only then could the malefactors be held in check and Los Angeles get a chance at a little culture.

Those wishes were partly honored in 1854, when the federal government authorized the establishment of a military post with the primary mission of "Indian control." Its location was not in Los Angeles, but more than forty miles due north, in the high tortured jumble of the Tehachapi Mountains, a transverse range that walls Southern California off from the rest of the state, and which some social historians have said marks a cultural barrier as well.

Fort Tejón took adobe form in a scenic calendar setting— as a well-watered, timbered little valley where grizzlies ambled among great-girthed oaks and domesticated beasts fed on tall, green grass. Close by were small lakes prodigally filled with fish by nature, a strategic mountain pass that descended into California's great Central Valley, and the Sebastian Indian Reservation that had been newly created out of chiefly humanitarian considerations. Indian unrest had plagued the southern San Joaquin Valley in the early 1850s. That it was brought on by crooked Indian agents and pushy miners and settlers was not unknown in Washington. Thus, the decision to establish the military post and the Indian reservation was meant more to protect the red man from the white, than vice versa.

Upright folks in Los Angeles did not care to dwell overly long on the government's reasons for sending soldiers. They were just pleased and honored that they were there, and they soon took a fancy to Lieutenant Colonel B.L. Beall, the "affable and courteous" base commander widely respected for his "liberality and munificence." The protection afforded by the bluecoats aside, the civilian social elite took a special delight in entertaining well-connected young officers from the East and civilization. There was always the chance that it might rub off.

Fort Tejón became the home of the dashing First Dragoons, a unit of proud and worthy horse soldiers that would later evolve into the illustrious First Cavalry Division, mechanized. They could have ridden right out of a John Ford movie. Their single-breasted blue frock coats fell well below their waists, their sky-blue trousers, trimmed on the side in orange cord, felt the constant rub of saddle leather and absorbed the lather of their mounts during the endless patrols and pursuits after rustlers and renegades and bandit gangs. They were proficient at their jobs, at home in their picturesque mountain post. Order of a kind had come to Southern California. But it was order of a surface kind, shortly to be violently broken.

The Friday morning of January 9, 1857 arrived cold and clear, and with a reveille sans bugle: at 6:30 the earth sighed and heaved under the bunks of the troopers. Nothing unusual about that. Minor earthquakes had been a regular part of camp life in the few years the army had been there.

Lt. Col. Beall was not among the early risers. Perhaps the "perks of rank" kept him in bed. But at precisely 8:33 the earth surged from beneath his bed and he sprang to his feet and plunged out the door of his adobe quarters, narrowly escaping a braining from falling plaster.

Outside, he staggered as he would on the deck of a violently pitching ship and watched with his astonished men as the unbelievable happened: the quartermaster's storehouse, the hospital, the officers' quarters, the barracks—all thirteen of the fort's buildings—either disintegrating or being knocked about at crazy angles. Accompanying the crash of falling roofs and walls were the terrified neighs and bleats of their livestock, and sharp cracking sounds as the trunks of the massive-bolled oak trees were sheared off just above the ground, as though they were the driest saplings.

The convulsion lasted a full two minutes, then subsided. Miraculously, Beall and his men had come through the ordeal without a death or a serious injury. But with the first aftershocks, reports from the neighboring region began filtering in: the Sebastian Indian Reservation was hard hit with many injured; a Mexican woman's head had been crushed in the collapse of a ranchhouse; a multitude of fish had been thrown out of the lakes to rot on the land; a circular corral had assumed the shape of an "S" with the sharp lateral shift of the ground; great fissures had opened in the earth—one had entombed a cow and another, twenty feet wide and forty miles long, had opened and then slammed shut with enough force to create a ridge ten feet wide and several feet high and yet another belched great dust clouds into the sky, leading the soldiers to believe that a "powerful volcanic eruption" was in progress just a couple of miles southwest of the battered fort.

The whole country seemed to be coming apart at the seams!

Much of Los Angeles was breakfasting that frosty January morning. Diners felt their tables gently rock at first, then vibrate with mounting force. Screaming and shrieking, tripping and tumbling over one another, they rushed from the Bella Union Hotel and other hostelries into the streets, where they were joined by near-naked bathers and dazed late-risers. What they saw was amazing. The land surface had the appearance of a field of wheat bending before a brisk wind blowing from north to south. The Los Angeles River was sloshing from side to side, then it jumped entirely out of its bed, forming pools that were driven madly about by the rocking earth. The cracking of building walls was echoed by the crash of falling merchandise from store shelves. Then the shaking ceased. Temporarily.

The first aftershock arrived at 11 A.M., but there were many more to follow in the afternoon and evening. And on that chilly January night, many Angelenos chatted excitedly around bonfires built in the street rather than return to their fractured domiciles. Nature had put on a smashing good show, it was agreed. Luckily the force of the temblor had spent itself over a full two minutes and not come all at once, or else, it was also agreed, there might not have been enough Angelenos left to bury the dead. As it was, only one life had been lost. An old man heading for the Plaza Church pitched to the earth, never to rise again, apparently a victim of heart failure.

East of Los Angeles, more severe effects were felt. Mission San Gabriel absorbed heavy damage. Men and horses in El Monte were knocked down in their fields. Wells in San Bernardino—where a "terrible report" issued from the mountains to the north—yielded water white as milk.

Meanwhile, some fifty miles north of San Bernardino and one-hundred miles east of the presumed epicenter near Fort Tejón, a lone surveyor was camped in the desert. William Denton, Esquire, was just finishing breakfast on the dry bed of the Mojave River when he heard a "peculiar harsh grating noise," immediately followed by simultaneous "vertical and oscillatory" movements that lasted forty seconds. With difficulty, he stayed on his feet. Then from the northwest came a thunderous roar "accompanied by the grinding of rocks and the crashing of mountains."

Denton's observations support the deductions of future generations of seismologists: namely, that the San Andreas Fault, in its binding dogleg course along Southern California's transverse mountain ranges, had suddenly released probably centuries of pent-up strain. The slow compilation of other contemporary reports have led some seismologists to conclude that the so-called Fort Tejón quake may have been the greatest to rock California since the advent of the white man. It was felt from Sacramento to San Francisco to Fort Yuma. Houses fell as far away as San Diego, and northwestern Mexico got a shaking. The Mokulumne River in the Central Valley jumped its banks, the Kern River was seen to flow upstream for a while.

Somewhat closer to ground zero, some artesian wells in the Santa Clara Valley abruptly went dry, while others bubbled to life. And from a mountainside in the San Fernando Valley, steaming gasses hissed from a vent surrounded by rocks hot to the touch, and farther down the mountain Indians reported seeing mysterious lights in the night from which they kept a wary distance.

Though the mountains around Fort Tejón continued to tremble for the next few years, the First Dragoons, temporarily quartered in tents, went right back to their high-riding heroics as they rebuilt their post. In Los Angeles, the excitement died down even sooner, the disturbance followed by one of a more familiar kind: less than two weeks after the earthquake, Sheriff Jim Baker rode south out of town with a posse of four deputies and a guide to bring in the celebrated bandit-revolutionary Juan Flores and his gang. Where he rode was into Juan's ambush that left Baker and three deputies dead of multiple gunshot wounds; the two survivors made it back to town, in panic, with an escort of bullets.

The outrage was too much even for Angelenos to take in stride. The Los Angeles *Star* shrilly called on all men of backbone to cleanse the civic honor with outlaw blood, and soon small armies of both Californios and gringos were scouring Southern California's hills and valleys. In eight days the outlaws were all hunted down, most of them executed on the spot, some of them shorn of their ears, which made eye-catching necklaces for macho vigilantes. As for the formidable Juan Flores, he was returned to town where, with a minimum of legal formality and some sloppy gallows building, he was made to twist slowly in the afternoon wind on a rope's end.

The Wild West days of frontier Los Angeles are mercifully gone, recalled only occasionally in the pulp magazines. But even less well-remembered is the Fort Tejón quake of 1857, for which the written accounts remain few and fragmentary. But still there are portions of a 225-mile scar in the earth's crust to remind the interested what can happen when the San Andreas Fault has a mind to move.

Then, the population of all Southern California was a few scattered thousand. Today more than fourteen million are crowded into the same area. Any repeat of the Fort Tejón event—which is not at all unlikely—would do more than take two lives, confuse a lot of cows and crumple some adobes. The toll would be appalling. Unthinkable.

3

THE MOUNTAIN BUILDER

The Owens Valley is a stunning feature of California's seldom-seen backside, a place where men's high hopes have folded and nature still deals in superlatives. To the west of the long valley is the crowning pride of the Golden State, the granitic Sierra Nevada, thick, brawny, young, and growing. To the east are the tandem Inyo and White Mountain ranges, steep, thin, bleak, sedimentary, and mature. And to the near southeast are the never-in-summer, scorched depths of Death Valley.

In the White Mountains grow the oldest living things on earth—the bent and tortured Bristlecone pines, sucking a few needles of life out of desiccative high ground. In Death Valley is the lowest spot in North America, the Badwater Sink, at −282 feet, and from there one can look west to the Sierra Nevada and see the highest peak in the conterminous United States, Mount Whitney at 14,495 feet.

Owens Valley cowers in this vise grip of mountain walls on troubled ground. Cinder cones and lava flows bespeak a volcanic past, and both old and recent scarps betray the presence of an active longitudinal fault that runs down most of its one-hundred-mile length.

White men arrived in this out-of-the-way scenic rift in the 1860s, lured by a siren call as old as greed: minerals. A rapid-fire series of gold and silver strikes brought them running, the all-or-nothing adventurers, the last-chancers, the temperate and the trigger-happy, the desperados and the dreamers. And in the colorful tradition of the West's great mining era, they settled in such boom-to-bust camps as Kearsarge, Chrysopolis, and wide-open, silver-heavy Cerro Gordo.

As was soon discovered, the Owens Valley had more to offer

than just rich ore. The land, watered by a network of rushing Sierra streams that generally merged to form the south-flowing Owens River, was passably fertile beyond the basaltic outcrops and the stands of stunted sagebrush. Both farmers and cattlemen joined the miners' rush to the ancestral home of the Paiute Indians

However well the white men thought of this high and dry land, the Paiutes prized the valley more, for the unarguable reason that it was theirs, the only home they could remember having had. And with a pride that compensated for their material poverty, they resisted the invasion and went on the warpath.

The scenario for the winning of the West was followed in detail. Indian obstinacy was countered with gunfire, which engendered massacres and mutilation, which were then returned in kind. On cue, the United States Army arrived and set up camp at Fort Independence, where well-intentioned junior officers got caught in a moral squeeze, rationalizing their siding with the encroaching settlers as not-quite-right but historically inevitable.

After nearly ten years of two-way atrocities, the Paiute War wound down. A relative calm prevailed over the settlements of Lone Pine, Independence, Coso, Bishop, Laws, and other communities that can now be located only on old maps. The mayhem tended to gravitate south, to Satan's own den, Cerro Gordo, where the high-spirited on a toot, having no appreciable number of redskins to shoot, amused themselves by shooting each other.

In high, arid lands, when the night sky is clear and the wind is stilled, the feeling of cold is delayed, yet goes bone deep. It was that kind of night in the Owens Valley during the early Tuesday morning hours of March 26, 1872. Overhead a moon just past full silvered the stringbean valley and gave it a look as lunar as the source of that reflected light. At 2:24 A.M. most miners and farmers were asleep in their homely make-do towns, but the silence of the early spring morning was then broken by a tremendous roar described as like a massive, rapid-fire artillery barrage accompanied by the clatter of musketry, coming from the Sierra Nevada west of Lone Pine. A convulsion of the earth raced eastward across the valley with the sound.

Sleeping Lone Pine stood, ever so briefly, directly in harm's way. Some of the town's 250-odd inhabitants died violently in their sleep as their adobe and stone homes collapsed above their beds. Others reeled drunkenly among falling walls and crashing timbers and got outside, where the din swelled with the rumble of mountain landslides, the howling of dogs and the lowing of cattle.

The first shock was variously reported as lasting from one to three minutes, at the end of which the town lay flat. Before the first aftershock at 6:30 A.M., survivors were attending to grisly necessities: Lone Pine's dead, to number twenty-two, were laid out in the local blacksmith shop. The sixty-odd injured were removed to the barroom of the Orleans Hotel, a wood-frame building that had, ironically, withstood the shock.

Lone Pine's casualty list—totaling a third of the inhabitants— leaves a remarkable record of the racial, national and occupational makeup of a typical early California mining camp. Among the dead and injured were Mexican and Chilean miners, Anglo-American merchants, two French frontiersmen, two sporting house ladies, an Irish girl and a German brewer's child, anonymous drifters, and a disproportionate number of infants. Curiously, the loss of human life was minimal beyond Lone Pine. At Independence, only a dozen miles to the north, where the unpopular two-story county courthouse tumbled down and saved a wrecker's bill, no one perished—though the mill superintendent of the nearby Eclipse Mine was crushed in his house and died in his wife's arms. A few miles farther north, near Camp Independence, which suffered near-total destruction of its thick adobe billets, only the baby of a farmer's wife died, suffocated under a pile of debris.

From still farther up the valley, at Bishop, came some comic relief. It seems not everyone was in bed that crisp, spring morning. One young blade had taken his ladylove out to view the moon and do some sparking. He hadn't drawn much fire before the big shock hit, according to an account in the Inyo *Independent*. But when it did, "the young lady, as in duty bound, fainted away. Our Adonis held her in his arms until she recovered, which required many minutes. The next day, he swore he would give $20 a shot for earthquakes when setting up with an offish gal."

The *Independent* remains the primary source for the human side of the earthquake story, and in its own right is an example of the frontier newspaper at its classic best. Salty and literate, it could also give valuable space to doggerel, as it did to W.H. Creighton and his poem that gave a folksy summation of the "Quake of '72":

Yes, stranger! we had a leettle shake
Here, and all 'round Lone Pine;
'Peared to me as like old Phosphorous
Had charge of the helm for a time.
It warn't no common shock, you bet!
Not one of your wavy kind,
But licket-y-split and rattle-ty-bang,
Just which way it had a mind.
Houses throwed down? You'd best believe!
There warn't a 'dobe wall
Nor yet a stone one, more'n one foot high,
That didn't have to fall;
It throwed the bottoms clean from under,
And crumpled the walls to dust,
And them as was sleepen' twixt 'dobe walls
Was them as fared the wust.
Anyone killed? Why where you bin,
That you ain't heerd the news?
How women and young'ins and men lay dead
In ones and threes and twos?
You see, 'twas two o'clock at night,
And them as received their call
Never knowed what struck 'em, or if they did
They hadn't no time to squall!
How many was dead? Well, twenty-five,
As near as we could count;
But some of the wounded and sick and maimed
Would likely swell that amount.
There's a man lives eighteen miles from here,
When it shook his old caboose,
"Get up old woman," said he to his mate,
"For I guess that hell's broke loose."
And, I reckon, that was how most of us felt,
Tho we all wasn't so profane,
For it shook and shook and rattled and tore
S'tho 'twould never be still again.
At Swansea, the lake went out from its banks
A good half-mile or more,
And when it cum back, 'twas tho' the devils in hell
Had joined in the awful roar.
How did I get out? Well, stranger, now
You've got me there, I swear;
The hole I cum thro'—it couldn't be found,
And I reckon it wasn't there.

I only know that I'm here today,
Lookin' over this desolate sand,
And I only hope He'll deal kindly with them
As is gone to the unknown land.

So much for the lighter and brighter side of the news. While the final toll of twenty-seven lives fell miraculously short of first expectations, the cost in property destroyed was high and widespread. Adobe and stone structures the length of the valley were leveled or made unsafe. Mine shorings were weakened, stamp-mill machinery hauled at great expense into the remote diggings became inoperative. Initial estimates of loss, made in the first bloom of postquake excitement, soared above $250,000, only to be revised downward later by the *Independent* and put the rival towns of Lone Pine and Independence at each others' civic throats.

Whatever dislocations beset man's enterprise in the sparsely settled valley, they were minor alongside the physical changes on the face of the earth. Numerous fissures rent the valley, most of them parallel to the mountain ranges, but some also cutting across diagonally. Between them the soil often collapsed dramatically, ponds forming in some depressions, others made dry, the ground churned and pulverized, as though some divine plow had momentarily descended to earth. One slump near Big Pine measured up to three-hundred feet across, leaving sheer vertical walls on both sides up to thirty feet high.

The life-sustaining Owens River, sixty to eighty feet wide where it bordered Independence, went abruptly dry for six hours after the temblor, then resumed its flow, only to select some new channels and leave the community of Bend City without a river for its bend. Lakelets vanished, others just as miraculously appeared.

Perhaps the most spectacular show of nature occurred at Owens Lake, now dry, but then a ten-mile-wide body of water at the south end of the valley. A family living at Swansea on the northeast edge of the lake, roused by the thunder of the quake, ran outside their house and were astonished to find the lake-bottom bare. The waters now reared in a perpendicular wall running lengthwise down the center of the seventeen-mile-long lake. There they roiled indecisively. The family was more decisive and immediately ran for higher ground, of which there was little for miles. The wall collapsed and the seismic seiche (as such freshwater standing waves are called) did race back for shore, but lapped only two-hundred gradually sloped feet beyond the old shoreline, doing little damage.

For two days, a thick cloud of dust hovered over the fractured valley as the aftershocks began, eventually to number, by one account, in excess of a thousand. Many triggered crashing landslides in the Sierra Nevada; friction from the falling granite was responsible for the "streams of fire" widely reported by awed observers. The detritus of broken rock choked some canyons and opened new paths for cascading Sierra streams, altering previous patterns of erosion, giving the land a new face.

The giant Owens Valley quake jarred the West beyond California. It was felt in Oregon, throughout Nevada, as far away as Salt Lake City and deep into Mexico. There were no seismographs then to record its shock waves. But by backward extrapolation of reported intensities felt over 640,000 square miles, some seismologists have estimated its magnitude as high as 8.3 on the Richter Scale, which would make it the biggest quake to have struck the West in historic times—if you exclude the Alaska shock of 1964, which measured 8.4.

Most all Californians swayed with it, of course. And generally speaking, the closer to Lone Pine the dizzier you got. One man who wasn't in Lone Pine but apparently experienced the maximum effects was the great naturalist John Muir, then living in his beloved Yosemite Valley, on the other side of the mountains from the epicenter. Muir was awakened by the quake and ran from his cabin into the moonlight, both frightened and elated, shouting to himself and the trees and the heavens, "A noble earthquake! A noble earthquake!" What followed he describes in his own soaring prose:

> I feared that the sheer-fronted Sentinel Rock, towering above my cabin, would be shaken down, and I took shelter back of a large yellow pine, hoping it might protect me from at least the smaller outbounding boulders. For a minute or two the shocks became more and more violent—flashing horizontal thrusts mixed with a few twists and battering, explosive, upheaving jolts—as if Nature were wrecking her Yosemite temple, and getting ready to build a still better one. . . . The Eagle Rock on the south wall, about a half mile up the valley, gave way and I saw it falling in thousands

24

of the great boulders I had so long been studying,
pouring to the Valley floor in a free curve, luminous
from friction, making a terribly sublime spectacle—an
arc of glowing, passionate fire, fifteen hundred feet
span, as true in form and as serene in beauty as a rain-
bow in the midst of the stupendous, roaring rock-storm.
The sound was so tremendously deep and broad and
earnest, the whole earth like a living creature seemed at
last to have found a voice and to be calling to her sister
planets. . . .

It seems almost ironic that Muir's grand words were not ad-
dressed to California's grand fault, the famous San Andreas. They
belonged to the action of a shorter, local rupture in the lithosphere
known, appropriately enough, as the Owens Valley Fault. California has more than one giant in its earth, and the one that moved
in 1872 moved mountains. Relative to the Owens Valley floor, the
Sierra Nevada had leaped as high as twenty-three vertical feet
and slid laterally north to a maximum of eighteen feet. And what
Muir and the shaken frontiersmen over the hill had witnessed was
a classic spasm in the normally drawn-out process geologists call
orogenesis, or mountain building.

Frontier-hardened survivors went on to better things following
the Great Shake of '72. Initial fears that the ruined Camp Independence would be abandoned and the miners left to the mercy of
renegade Indian bands were eased when the federal government
chose to rebuild the post. But what the earth on a rampage had
failed to put asunder, men in their day-to-day competition were
prepared to dismember.

A certain Colonel Charles Whipple, who narrowly escaped with
his life from the second story of his home when the first tremor
struck and brought it down, caught the first stage west out of
Lone Pine. With him he took the hopes of the stricken towns-
people. His mission? To spread the sad tidings. And to solicit alms
from those of means in San Francisco and Los Angeles.

Colonel Whipple was a born fund-raiser, it seems. His tales of
woe loosened tear ducts and purses in San Francisco, where at
least $4,000 in relief were subscribed, to go with the $2,200 collected in Visalia, Swansea, and from the big-hearted, shoot-'em-up
fellows at lightly hit Cerro Gordo. (Los Angelenos, apparently
having given at the office, sent only $840 and letters of sympathy.)

Word of Whipple's coastal success crested the Sierra Nevada

25

and reached Independence, where the begging on behalf of neighboring Lone Pine was not taken kindly. Damage reports were highly exaggerated, sniffed the proud *Independent*. Lone Pine was claiming property losses of more than double what the town was worth. What the valley needed were not handouts, but credit and confidence in its mineral potential. Besides, what could Colonel Whipple know of the true state of affairs, since he had caught the first stage out of the valley, in darkness, less than two hours after the first tremor? Whipple's neighbors in hard-hit Lone Pine cancelled their subscriptions to the *Independent* and started reading the Visalia *Delta*.

The trauma soon healed and men went back to their mines and mining districts, and the valley again prospered as the burrowers extracted their precious metals, leaving tailings to be mined when they were gone. For a time. The truism has it that God in His inscrutable wisdom invariably puts riches in the bleakest, most inhospitable of places. Another truism, verified over and over in America's mountainous West, is that the coveted ores are finite and do play out. Then men and women and their children reliant upon assayers' reports and smelter receipts move on, leaving behind emptied glory holes and their rude homes to weather and crumble.

The Owens Valley had its ghost towns early on. But it also had a fine river and a water supply that promised an agricultural future. For a while, anyway. In the second decade of this century the rapidly growing city of Los Angeles developed a great thirst. What it wanted then, and later, and now, was water. And what Los Angeles wants, Los Angeles gets, one way or another.

As the Owens Valley smelters were belching their last, agents from the southern metropolis began buying up water rights to the Owens River. Once the news of the grab got around, the situation grew tense and would remain so for nearly two decades. Local farmers from time to time grabbed their guns and went to the barricades, even dynamited sections of the water system. But it was a case of too little and too late. Warring against Los Angeles is like playing roulette in Las Vegas—the odds are definitely not with you. The clean-tasting water melted of Sierra snows was flowing into the San Fernando Valley in 1913 and has been doing so ever since.

The war is not quite over, however, as was dramatically demonstrated again in September of 1976 when the aqueduct was dynamited again and $6 million damage was done to the Los Angeles water system. The city's newer taxpayers were puzzled by this seemingly senseless act of destruction in the Owens Valley. But then they're less versed in California history than their own Department of Water and Power.

Today, winter skiers and summer campers bound for the Sierra Nevada's bountiful rear end stop for gas and burgers in Lone Pine, Independence and Bishop. If they had a mind to talk (which they generally don't) with the aged gas-pumper or fry-cook serving them, they might open an unexpected vein of bitterness. An old-timer who still remembers will tell you that the valley has known better days, that the increased siphoning of "their" water by Los Angeles has turned the Owens Valley into a dustbowl, making it old before its time. The austere earth, if it had a tongue, would contradict them. It would say that the Sierra Nevada is still young and still growing.

4

THAT WAS
THE CITY THAT WAS

It was the best of towns, it was the worst of towns; but to those 400,000 lively souls who called themselves San Franciscans in the spring of 1906, it wasn't a town at all. It was the City. Not just any city. But The City! The only city.

Parisians, Romans, Londoners, not to mention New Yorkers, might dismiss the presumption as a provincial expelling of so much youthful hot air. They would have been partly right. The City by the Golden Gate was young and brash. And cocksure. And self-indulgent. A wide-open, anything-goes, teeming city of crazy-running streets that climbed up and careened down a hundred hills and could have been laid out by a drunken drayer on some wild night's spree.

Yet San Francisco was anything but provincial. Perhaps no city in human history was as instantaneously and marvelously cosmopolitan or polyglot as Bagdad by the Bay. Will Irwin, in his *City That Was,* a moving obituary written even as his beloved hometown was burning to the ground, describes its people in all their genetic diversity. There were the proud descendents of Spanish hidalgos who had founded the settlement in the year 1776, and the more numerous descendents of mestizos who built it. Sons and daughters of argonauts who had heeded the call of '49 and arrived from most everywhere. A later sprinkling of educated Frenchmen. Then a tide of Italians, many of them Neapolitans who sailed their fishing fleets out of the Golden Gate under triangular lateen sails, as their fathers had in the old country. Then the Irish; some of them led west by the railroads they built, some of them—those with the smiles and the charm—drawn into San Francisco politics where the boodle was. Industrious, taciturn Germans. Blacks whose past was in the South and in bondage.

29

Talented, mercantile Jews. The Chinese who had been brought in as forced labor and shrunk into the cramped confines of six-block-long, two-block-wide Chinatown, objects of hatred by lower-class whites. And the law-abiding, hard-working Japanese who knew the same unrelenting discrimination.

No one people stayed pure at this glorious end of the earth. Intermarriage was common, the fusing of bloods without religious or civil ceremony was not unknown. Nor did the mixing end there. Exotic peoples in lesser numbers turned up at the noisy hell of the Barbary Coast: stocky Russian sailors, beturbaned Lascars, Kanakas from Hawaii, Indians from Alaska, black Gilbert Islanders, Greeks, Filipinos . . . to name just a few that brought zest and occasional rowdiness to the port that served the world.

Sober Easterners were horrified by what went on in San Francisco right up to April of 1906. City government was an open scandal; king-maker Abraham Ruef, a French Jew, and his handpicked mayor, Eugene Schmitz, an Irish German, handled the patronage and the swag. Prostitution was rampant, with cribs to match all tastes and pocketbooks. Barbary Coast fun came cheap and quick for visiting sailors, while Chinatown catered mostly to its own. In the Tenderloin district, French restaurants upheld the lofty traditions of the world's finest cuisine on the first floor; upstairs quite different tastes were served in a high-toned atmosphere. And since the city had no closing laws, good times were available twenty-four hours a day, seven days a week.

Opium dens were also still around, dispensing pills and gum to incurable dreamers. Outside, on the night streets, the pace of life was quicker, enlivened by knifings, shootings, and plain honest brawls. And although the heydays of shanghaiing were over, a tipsy fellow wandering the waterfront could still get bopped by a crimp and wake up the next morning on a ship bound for Singapore.

San Franciscans resented outside criticism of their lives and their live-and-let-live ways. They didn't cotton much to gentility and swells' put-on airs. Without self-doubts, they thought of themselves as the gayest, most lighthearted, fun-loving people around. And anyone who didn't agree could go hang. Will Irwin prefaces his book with a borrowed sentence that pungently captures the height of this civic pride. Said one Willie Britt, "I'd rather be a busted lamp post on Battery Street, San Francisco, than the Waldorf-Astoria."

Perhaps a city that owed its very existence to Mother Lode gold and Comstock silver came by its exuberance naturally. At the land's end of American westering, hope was redeemed and promises came true, and life by the beautiful bay with soft gray fogs could never be anything but gay. So it seemed on April 18, 1906.

San Francisco, lying just east of the San Andreas Fault, was no stranger to earthquakes. After Americans arrived in numbers at the gateway to the gold-fields, moderate to moderately heavy shocks rocked the city on an average of about once every three years. On the morning of October 21, 1868, a major shock thought to have been about seven on the Richter Scale rammed the city, bringing down walls that took five lives. This killer quake came not from San Andreas, curiously, but from the nervous Hayward Fault eighteen miles to the east, which runs as the big break's north-south parallel for some forty miles. Still, that wasn't a bad record . . . five lives lost in nearly sixty years. One could live with it. Even joke about the "shakers." Like the crisp Bay air, a little bouncing every now and then kept the spring in a man's step.

San Franciscans had a greater adversary to worry about. Fire. Six times during the first flush years of the Gold Rush, flames had consumed great chunks of the town. Each time it was rebuilt, predominantly of wooden structures rising shoulder-to-shoulder. That the city had escaped a major calamity over the next fifty years was due solely to its fire-fighters; at first they were public-spirited volunteers who formed rival companies and at a moment's notice quit their businesses and their beds to go clanging off on horse-drawn fire wagons to quench blazes. They were succeeded by civil employees who wrote a no-less-memorable chapter in the annals of American fire-fighting.

But San Francisco was living on borrowed time. That was the heavyweight opinion of the National Board of Fire Underwriters. In a report made public in October, 1905, the Board stated that the city had "violated all underwriting traditions and precedents by not burning up. That it has not already done so," the report went on, "is largely due to the vigilance of the Fire Department, which cannot be relied upon indefinitely to stave off the inevitable."

That sobering news came as no news at all to Fire Chief Dennis Sullivan. For thirteen years he had tried tirelessly and most futilely to head off disaster. He better than anyone knew the danger of fire to his growing city; the downtown skyline was sprouting with supposedly fireproof brick buildings, but most of the city—especially south of Market Street and west toward the Mission District—remained a tinderbox clutter of flimsy wood structures. Chief Sullivan also knew better than anyone that should the right match be applied, he and his department would be powerless to control the holocaust.

Sullivan's greatest handicap was an inadequate water supply. Most of what was available was piped from distant reservoirs, including one down the peninsula with a name that no Californian who lived after the chief was relieved of his earthly duties could hear without flinching, if just a little: Lake San Andreas. What if the mains were by some chance to break? Sullivan wanted to refill and reactivate the many old cisterns that underlay the city. He wanted a backup saltwater system that would tap the close-by ample supply in the Bay. He wanted to train his men in the use of dynamite to blast out mid-city firebreaks, if that became necessary. But all that required money, of course. And though the city wasn't hurting any, the bucks were earmarked for other projects and pockets. Even after the National Board of Fire Underwriters' chilling report was released, Sullivan had trouble budging City Hall. Mayor Eugene Schmitz put him off. He'd think about it. He'd have his citizen's advisory committee look into the matter. On April 17, 1906, the city's veteran and resourceful fire chief was a very frustrated man.

San Franciscans had a lot to talk about that fine spring day. Across the ocean another city built on a scenic bay was facing disaster. On April 6, angry Mount Vesuvius had blown its top again, and now a wall of lava was threatening Naples with extinction. Mayor Schmitz asked citizens to open their hearts and contribute to a relief fund that had been set up for the unfortunates. In Germany, Kaiser Wilhelm was making bellicose noises, but the poor man was not to be taken seriously, not really.

Closer to home, President Teddy Roosevelt had some unkind words for muckrakers. In turn, William Randolph Hearst's muckraking San Francisco *Examiner* had some unkind words for T.R., the pith of which seriously questioned the president's mental capacity.

But the big news and the best news on the seventeenth was even closer to home. The Metropolitan Opera was in town, as was

32

that tenor of tenors, the incomparable Enrico Caruso. San Franciscans had always loved the theater. Grand opera they loved best of all, and they prided themselves on their critical judgment. The previous night soprano Olive Fremstad had sung Goldmark's *Queen of Sheba* to decidedly down reviews. The city's trio of papers all expressed disappointment in the performers out from New York.

Caruso had sat that one out. But tonight he was due to face the music lovers as Don José in Bizet's *Carmen,* with Madame Fremstad singing the part of the cigarette factory lovely for the first time. San Franciscans savored theater gossip almost as much as theater itself. It was reported that Caruso had not wanted to come to San Francisco and had done so with the greatest reluctance. Which was true. It was said that the rotund Neapolitan was on the outs with the Grand Teuton Fremstad. Which was true. It was also said that the temperamental man was displeased with the critics' handling of the *Queen of Sheba* and was poised to show his best. Which also seems to have been true.

Caruso left his suite in the elegant Plaza Hotel that evening prepared to show the three-thousand people jammed into the Grand Opera House on Mission Street how to sing. And that is just what he did. The critics again found fault with Madame Fremstad: as a Carmen, she was a good Brünnhilde. But the great Caruso had wowed them and won them with his virtuosity, as their reviews would have certified had they appeared in the morrow's press.

The Tuesday evening was cool and pleasant right into early Wednesday morning. The gaiety of the night's celebrants was at its normal midweek pitch, and after midnight it began to subside, collect in small pockets of glass-tinkling and laughter that traveled far in the night air. All very normal. After midnight two fires broke out, one in North Beach and the other in a warehouse on Market Street. Both were put out, and a tired Chief Sullivan climbed back into bed near three o'clock. That too was normal.

Everything seemed about right in those early morning hours . . . except the noisy horses. In livery stables, fire stations and elsewhere they were making nuisances of themselves with their stomping and thrashing and neighing. And the city's dogs, too, were raising an awful racket. That was not normal. A change in the weather, maybe.

Precisely at 5:12 A.M. it arrived from the northwest, a giant

33

8.25-magnitude, rip-snorting earth-wrencher that freed the two locked walls along the San Andreas Fault. The floor of the city heaved, fell, and twisted, a "vertical and rotary" movement that mounted in intensity for forty endless seconds. Then came a ten-second pause of fool's hope. Then it struck again with even. greater ferocity, a frenetic dance that had the streets rolling in waves for another twenty-five terrifying seconds, before dying in a sputter of slight trailer shocks.

Its sound was described variously, but "a deep and terrible rumbling" seems to say it all. For a brief time, that is. The earth-noise was quickly masked by the cracking, groaning, and rasping of buildings that all too often ended in a roar of collapse. Throughout the city, older and weaker structures came down atop their sleeping occupants to a number that no one would ever precisely know. The four-story Valencia Hotel in the Mission District was but one of the big killers, yet an exception in that some of those who died—estimated as many as eighty—actually drowned: a broken water main had flooded the telescoped wreckage.

One of San Francisco's first casualties was the one man it could least afford to lose. The quake awoke Chief Dennis Sullivan and he bolted for his wife's room above the Bush Street fire station. He never made it. Smokestacks from the adjacent California Hotel had fallen and shorn away the wall of the station, and he hurtled three floors down to sprawl across a fire wagon, his skull fatally fractured, never to regain consciousness in the three days he lay in the Southern Pacific Hospital. A grievous loss that would haunt the city ever after.

The overwhelming majority of San Franciscans survived the quake, unnerved but intact. Some asleep were catapulted from their beds. Some early risers were thrown right back into them. Others were knocked to the floors of their rooms. Still others kept to their feet and managed to dodge sliding bureaus and tables which the earth turned on them.

When the earth stilled, San Franciscans, many in their nightclothes, began to cluster in the streets. Save for the moans and cries of the injured under the scattered rubble heaps, the silence was eerie, and the survivors spoke in sober whispers, as if they were in church. Then gradually, spirits brightened with the day, which dawned blue and clear above the Berkeley Hills across the Bay.

Some of the more curious walked up the city's hills to better survey the damage, see it in panorama. What they saw were plumes of smoke lazily climbing into the calm air, mere wisps of gray from fires that were still small, yet widespread. One had reason to worry about them if. . . .

Brigadier General Frederick Funston had a short walk from his quarters to the top of Nob Hill. What he saw he didn't like at all. General Funston was a bantam-size, hard-beaked warrior, a national hero for his exploits in putting down the Philippine insurrection against U.S. imperial control in the days following the Spanish American War. Assigned to San Francisco in 1901, he remained a man of action, and one of very strong feelings. He had come to love The City. He was fond of Chief Sullivan, a worthy man. But he despised Schmitz and his grafting cronies and the license they allowed to flourish. That kind couldn't stand up to a first-class emergency, and from where he stood and from what he saw, that was exactly what was building in those thickening columns of smoke.

Major General Adolphus Greeley, Commander of the Pacific Division, was out of town that day, leaving Funston the ranking army officer in the city, and the man of action acted decisively, well before seven o'clock, when the rifle-toting troops he ordered from Fort Mason arrived on Market Street; by eight A.M. the number of "boys in blue" had swelled to 1,700 with armed reinforcements from the Presidio. What Funston had done, or would shortly do, was to quite illegally and unconstitutionally impose de facto martial law on San Francisco. And the events of the next days would suck him into the storm center of a controversy that swirls still.

Funston's reason for doing as he did was straightforward enough. He had watched fire wagons rush to a blaze, hook their hoses to hydrants, and turn on the valves. A trickle, and then nothing. The mains were busted. That meant the fat was in the fires—of which there were several—and spreading. Only he and his troops could save the city.

There were other cities as well as towns and hamlets strung out along the 270 miles of the San Andreas Fault that split open on the April morning. They felt the same blow as San Francisco. Some felt it more severely, and sooner. Eureka and Fort Bragg in

35

the north got the shakings of their lives, and damage was severe; the latter's famous Russian church was knocked to splinters. Sebastapol also took the brunt of it. So did Tomales, where two were killed. At Point Reyes a locomotive and four commuter cars were knocked flat off the track and on their sides into a bed of poppies, but miraculously no one was even injured.

At Santa Rosa fate had cheated the other way. Although the Sonoma Valley community was situated nineteen miles east of the San Andreas Fault, the combination of soft alluvial soil and poorly braced buildings bonded by defective mortar helped bring the town's bricks down, to be immediately enveloped in raging fires. Given the differences in population, the more than fifty lives lost at Santa Rosa would make its tragedy even greater than San Francisco's.

South of the Golden Gate, the picture wasn't any brighter alongside the San Andreas Fault, which in its shearing ripped the earth's surface all the way to Salinas. Damage to Peninsula towns ran into the millions of dollars, and young Stanford University, with fourteen buildings down, was a perfect shambles. William James, the great American philosopher-psychologist, happened to be temporarily in residence on the Farm and left us a singular record of how the clear, inquiring mind confronts catastrophe:

> When . . . I felt the bed begin to waggle, my first consciousness was one of gleeful recognition of the nature of the movement. "By Jove," I said to myself, "here's B's old earthquake, after all!" And then it went *crescendo,* "and a jolly good one it is, too!" I said.
>
> Sitting up involuntarily, and taking a kneeling position, I was thrown down on my face as it went *fortior* shaking the room exactly as a terrier shakes a rat. Then everything that was on anything else slid off to the floor, over went bureau and chiffonier with a crash, as the *fortissimo* was reached; plaster cracked, an awful roaring noise seemed to fill the outer air, and in an instant all was still again. . . .
>
> [My] emotion consisted wholly of glee and admiration; glee at the vividness which such an abstract idea or verbal term as "earthquake" could put on when translated into sensible reality and verified concretely; and admiration at the way in which the frail wooden house could hold itself together in spite of the shaking.

I felt no trace whatever of fear; it was pure delight and welcome.

"Go it," I almost cried aloud, "and go it stronger!"

The quake had already gone strong enough. From the famous pragmatist's words one would never guess that the University suffered $5 million in damage. Nor that two people had the life crushed out of them—and that there were not more was only because classes were not in session.

Farther south the horrors mounted. Reports of death and destruction filtered slowly out of such distant towns as Monterey, Salinas, Hollister. But the focal point of the earth's fury was San Jose, then called by some "The Prettiest City in California." That it was not after 5:12:45 A.M. on April 18. Every building of brick or stone over two stories high was either leveled or ready for the wrecking crews. Nineteen people perished.

For a spot just outside San Jose, nature reserved its cruelest blow: the four-story Agnews State Insane Asylum, where more than a thousand inmates and staff were housed, collapsed with a deafening roar. When rescuers arrived on the ghastly scene, they found uncontrolled hysteria and one demented survivor repeating over and over, "Jesus of Nazareth is passing." They dug one-hundred-nineteen dead and dying out of the ruins, including Superintendent Kelly and his wife, and eleven nurses. For a time, area residents fretted about the lunatics who had escaped and were roaming the countryside, but all were eventually rounded up without incident.

In its long, narrow, punishing path the quake had killed by crushing, by drowning, by fire. In the far south, at a place called Hinckley Gulch, it chose yet another means. Nine men were working in a sawmill set in the narrow gorge. The earth shuddered, and tons of canyon wall came screeching down to bury them alive.

To name a major earthquake after one city or locale always slights those who suffer equally at the fringes. But in the case of San Francisco, the name seems deserved. Most of the towns and cities in the swath of destruction had faced havoc for minutes, perhaps hours in fighting the after-fires. The City, stripped of its defenses in a minute and a half, now had to undergo its own ordeal by fire—and that was to last for four days.

General Funston and Mayor Schmitz formed a strained and temporary alliance on Wednesday morning, when the smoke could still be distinguished as rising from scattered blazes; and the mayor showed that his spine wasn't just spaghetti with a proclamation as sternly worded as any order Funston would give:

> The Federal Troops, the members of the Regular Police Force and all Special Police Officers have been authorized by me to KILL any and all persons found engaged in Looting or in the Commission of Any Other Crime.
>
> I have directed all the Gas and Electric Lighting Co.'s not to turn on Gas or Electricity until I order them to do so. You may therefore expect the city to remain in darkness for an indefinite time.
>
> I request all citizens to remain at home from darkness until daylight every night until order is restored.
>
> I WARN all Citizens of the danger of fire from Damaged or Destroyed Chimneys, Broken or Leaking Gas Pipes or Fixtures, or any like causes.

His honor also ordered all the city saloons closed, an act that underscores just how grave the situation was in a city famous then and now for the unquenchable thirst of its citizens.

Both General and Mayor took to the streets, and there they fought the fires, hour by hour, street by street. Their battle, though valiant, was a losing one, as became increasingly clear when the morning's fires swelled. Below Market Street, in the district known as South of the Slot, a series of small blazes united into an inferno that raced through a crowd of wretched dry-wood structures. From the west it was joined by the "Ham-and-Eggs" fire, so named for the late breakfast a woman was preparing when her chimney caught fire and spread flames through thirty blocks.

Meanwhile, north of Market Street, downtown, a third conflagration burned out of control as high-rise, fireproof buildings became tall torches, igniting their street-mates, which burned their way from the top floors down.

Fire-fighters tried to stay the advancing flames with the little water they could find—in old cisterns, in the city's sewers. Hopeless. They also tried dynamiting blocks of buildings to make inner city firebreaks, but explosives in inexperienced hands made matters worse. Blasting only reduced buildings to convenient tinder piles for the onroaring fires, or hurled flaming debris into blocks unburned.

By Wednesday midnight most of San Francisco's famed landmarks were gutted or reduced to ashes and black forests of skeletal steel. Chinatown was no more. The Grand Opera House had burned, as had the Palace Hotel, which a temporarily deranged Enrico Caruso vacated in time.

Most San Franciscans who rubbernecked Wednesday morning, and passively watched as fire-fighters and troops fell back from the fires, knew by Thursday morning that the city was doomed. Then the exodus began in earnest. The Ferry Building at the foot of Market Street was a crush of flailing elbows as men, women and children jammed Oakland-bound boats for a haven. Among the afternoon passengers was Enrico Caruso, who vowed never to return to San Francisco, barely visible under a miles-high pall of smoke that blotted out the sunlight. It was a vow he kept.

On Thursday the Mission District was consumed by the southern arm of the fire. Meanwhile, north of Market, the unstoppable flames swept west and inched north. Gone with the red wind were the mansions of Nob Hill, the parvenu palaces built by the Central Pacific's Bonanza Kings—Leland Stanford, Charles Crocker, Mark Hopkins, Collis P. Huntington. Grander symbols of the City's wild and gaudy past could not have been found for the burning.

By early Friday morning, with a supreme effort that featured backfiring and artillery pieces firing point blank into buildings, and others blown up by a late-arriving, expert Navy demolition crew, the flames were halted in the west along the broad expanse of Van Ness Avenue. That was the good news. The bad news was that the fire was now spreading north, whipped along by a brisk west wind that, had it blown two days earlier, might have saved most of the city. For another day North Beach and environs took their turn fueling the flames, which north of Telegraph Hill burned right to the baywater. Finally, on Saturday morning the last flames were snuffed. The contest was over.

The winner, by a lopsided decision, was the fire born of the earthquake. It left 4.7 square miles of baked ruins, 490 blackened blocks. In its northeast-southwest swath remained two small slightly singed islands—half of Russian Hill and a few downtown blocks—and a peninsula at Telegraph Hill, where the Italian residents helped check the blaze by emptying their cellars and pouring barrels of red wine on the tongues of fire. And behind Telegraph Hill, in a heroic last stand, fire-fighters did manage to save most of the city's wharves and docks—its life line to the world.

No one will ever know exactly how many died in the two-phase disaster. Estimates range from a low of 450 all the way up to 1,000. The reasons are several: those whose thankless duty it was to collect corpses even as the city burned were told to cremate them for health reasons. This they did, in scattered spots, without the time or the mind to keep count, let alone report all to the coroner. Other victims, dead, dying, or merely trapped under fallen timbers, were cremated by the fire itself. Some of the unaccounted for had to be the loners, the friendless, the drifters who have always gravitated to cities for sanctuary.

The quake-fire left behind some bitterness to exacerbate the loss. Most centered on the actions of General Funston, and most particularly on those of his troops who were accused of being trigger-happy and callous in forcing residents from their homes many hours in advance of the fires that consumed their possessions. Summary executions by bullet and bayonet were said to have extended beyond out-and-out looters to panicky persons simply trying to return to their homes. Since those four days of confusion and suffering, some have down-played the whole subject of street shootings, but there were enough reliable eyewitness accounts to validate accusations. The same accounts insist that those killed—in the dozens, some calculate—included innocents as well as thugs and thieves.

General Funston stoutly defended his actions and those of his well-disciplined soldiers. The few incidents he had heard about, he claimed, were the responsibility of the militia called out by Mayor Schmitz. Indeed, the great majority of eyewitnesses had nothing but high praise for Funston's boys in blue. The militia, conversely, did not receive very high marks in conduct from anyone.

Instances of street violence in the stricken city remained rare and ugly exceptions to human behavior. The overwhelming majority were pictured as subdued, faces drawn after the first day, but orderly. William James, dedicated psychologist that he was, corroborates this. He took a train up the peninsula on April 18 to observe the "subjective phenomena" in San Francisco. When he arrived, he found its people in the streets, "busy as ants in an uncovered ant-hill scurrying to save their eggs and larvae." What surprised him was the purposefulness of the population, the lack of complaints, the downright cheerfulness of some who went about their sorry business.

"I heard not a single really pathetic or sentimental word in California expressed by anyone," he wrote. "The terms 'awful,' 'dreadful' fell often enough from people's lips, but always with a sort of abstract meaning, and with a face that seemed to admire the vastness of the catastrophe as much as it bewailed its cutting-ness."

James speculated that all this stoical optimism might be characteristic of Californians, and that it sprang from their educational system, which taught all ills were amenable to healing.

San Francisco "recuperated" in record time, thanks to the resiliency of its people. As the still-warm ashes were being carted off, business resumed, including the selling of souvenir rubble off the streets. In six weeks all the banks were open. A reconstruction committee was formed in a matter of days and diligently went about restoring vital services, as refugee camps were being built beyond the periphery of the burned area, including a big one in beautiful Golden Gate Park, where as many as 200,000 went just after the fire. In keeping with the general cleanup, Mayor Schmitz was indicted for taking bribes before the year was out, and Boss Abe Ruef did some time in San Quentin.

San Francisco came back so fast that by December of 1906 the city's fathers were planning the Panama-Pacific International Exposition that was to dazzle visitors from around the world in 1915. It was as if the earth had never shaken, the city never burned. There was, however, one lethal legacy that had to be reckoned with after the city got back on its feet. Rats. More to the point, rats freed to circulate through the water and sewer systems. The gifted photographer Arnold Genthe, who left a matchless pictorial record of the disaster, saw them chewing away at the limbs of corpses in Chinatown while the city still burned. The sight turned his stomach. Though Mayor Schmitz did his best to suppress the facts, more than 150 cases of bubonic plague were recorded in the months that followed the quake, and deaths occurred in all sections of the city, among all classes.

As resilient as San Franciscans proved themselves to be, recovery was not strictly a hometown miracle. The disaster stirred sympathy everywhere, and the city's many friends opened their purses. In addition to the nine million dollars in federal funds

41

dispensed through the American Red Cross, cities and organizations across the land sent their own dollars and relief trains. Most prominent among the givers was Los Angeles, most commonly thought of as a bitter rival of the metropolis to the north. Before the fire was sixteen hours old, a train from Los Angeles arrived with food and medical supplies and medical personnel; more aid would follow.

Help did not end at the nation's borders. Money arrived from abroad, from Europe, from Russia, from Dictator Porfirio Diaz's Mexico. But again the heaviest foreign contributor was a surprise: Japan, which sent nearly a quarter of a million dollars. True, the Japanese knew as well as anyone the agony of earthquakes; but it seems an unequaled act of charity when one remembers that their own people were so harshly treated in "The City."

San Francisco casts a spell on all those who have ever seen it. The city communicates sentiment as though it were contagious, borne on its creeping fogs. Like Paris, it is every romantic's home away from home, a good place well remembered. That's the way it was with The City That Was. That's the way it is with the city that is.

It would be nice to say that San Francisco learned its lesson in 1906. Nice, but hardly accurate.

Even before the San Andreas Fault came apart at the seam, some influential citizens had gone beyond talking about remodeling their chosen city. In 1904, they commissioned the highly regarded architect Daniel H. Burnham to draft a design for the beautification of San Francisco. Burnham gave them a plan which envisioned new and wider streets, better access to the municipal hills, and other conveniences tailored to swell civic pride. Nothing happened. Then when the quake struck and did the preliminary clearing work so completely, the Burnham Plan backers took heart and trumpeted the once-in-a-lifetime opportunity. Unfortunately, the headstrong plunged headlong into rebuilding, and what came of the rush was a mishmash that bore a striking resemblance to the city that was. The debris cleared away was dumped into the Bay to make more land just like the land that experienced the worst churning in '06.

San Francisco's population has doubled since its four-day chastening. Suburbs have mushroomed to provide more bed-

A statue of scientist Louis Agassiz, toppled from Stanford University's Geology Building, made a big hit on campus during the so-called San Francisco Quake of 1906.

rooms. One of them, Daly City by name, features homes built literally on top of the San Andreas rip. Instead of looking at the untrustworthy earth, San Francisco's powers that be chose to look up at the sky in the 1960s and early 1970s. They have erected the towering TransAmerica A-frame and lesser sky-scratchers plentifully faced in glass to maximize Bay-viewing. And in looking up and out they have forgotten that high-rises do not a city make. People do that, in the ambience and traditions they create—as they had already done in San Francisco quite well.

The city's new skyline conforms with the California Uniform Building Code, and it is designed to be earthquake resistant. That invites the question, which is not "What if?" but "When?" A giant quake of 8-plus magnitude is estimated to occur along the San Andreas Fault every hundred years, give or take a few decades. When the earth's crust next yields to the accumulated strain

43

that has been gathering since 1906, what then? Do all building guarantees go out the windows—right after the plate glass that will be raining down on city streets like so many thousands of guillotines?

No doubt San Francisco is an exciting city. But at some future, unspecified date, it is sure to push excitement beyond tolerable limits.

The city has taken some protective measures, to be sure. The Fire Department can now draw on several reinforced concrete reservoirs situated in the hills, more than a hundred refurbished and replenished cisterns under the city, and two saltwater pumping stations to tap the limitless waters of the Bay. They should come in handy.

San Francisco also has its Mayor's Office of Emergency Services, a five-man department headed by Edward Joyce. Joyce is a resourceful man who makes the most of his $174,000 annual budget. But he can only react to a disaster after the fact, not remake the city to better prepare it for same. Which again invokes the when-it-happens question. Loss assessments have been estimated for "the next big one," and the most liberal ones price another 8.25 earth-wrencher at 100,000 dead, 500,000 injured, and $25 billion in property loss.

As they say, it's a nice place to visit, but. . . .

5

A BLESSING
IN DISGUISE

If Californians were ever asked to vote on the state's most beautiful small city, and if the ballot were secret and Chamber of Commerce types barred from the polls, Santa Barbara would surely win by at least a comfortable plurality. It stands gracefully on its mesa base, flanked by a cobalt sea and florally luxuriant hills that in a few short miles become mountains.

The city itself has the look of a Mediterranean confection, carefully prepared within the high standards of American hygiene. Creamy stucco walls rise—not too high—to red-tile roofs that overlook streets with lyric Spanish names, and sidewalks are planted with an encyclopedic variety of palms, well-cropped hibiscus, magnolias, and enough other flowering imports to keep any amateur botanist in a state of rapture. All this loveliness converges upon, but is by no means confined to, State Street, or the Calle del Estado, the main drag that runs east-west through the cool and sunny coastal town.

And yet this modern concentration of college campuses, culture fans, and old wealth is not without its faults—at least three underlie Santa Barbara and its environs—and from time to time they make their presence felt. For as scenically splendid as the close conjunction of mountains and sea may be in nature, that same conjunction is often a reliable sign that one is in earthquake country.

Back in 1925, Santa Barbara had not yet become the Platonic vision of California that it is today. But it was trying. Or at least the powerful Community Arts Association—a group that one contemporary admirer saluted for its propensities toward "religion, romance, beauty, art"—was trying. No mention was made of money, but Santa Barbarans, who already included an influential body of retirees from the East, had a lot of that too, even then.

CALIFORNIA QUAKE

The Community Arts Association had made some progress in persuading residents to build in the eclectic "California Spanish style," which owed debts to the Moors, New Spain, and Italy, but was also distinctive and derived from the mission architecture of the early Spanish colonizers. In late June of 1925 the Association won a telling victory by getting the city to tighten its building code. But that, of course, could not be retroactively applied to the tawdry and tacky structures already standing, particularly to public eyesore number one, State Street, which bore a striking resemblance to some midwestern Main Street miraculously transported to Pacific shores.

The public-spirited members of the Community Arts Association had no way of knowing that their most powerful ally was the earth and that in a matter of a few days it would move on their behalf, along the Mesa Fault that practically underlay offensive State Street.

The early morning hours of June 29, 1925, were uncommonly hot, still, sultry—perfect "earthquake weather," as California folklore has it. At 3:27 A.M., pressure gauges of the municipal water system recorded slight disturbances in the earth, but nobody knew that, for the record hadn't been consulted. At about that time Herbert Nunn, Santa Barbara's City Manager, awakened at his beachside home and couldn't get back to sleep. The humidity was unbearable, but there was something else—a smell—the strong and offensive odor of crude oil. That was odd. Later he took a walk and found patches of oil had seeped up through the surface sand of nearly a mile stretch of beach. That hadn't happened before! Very strange goings-on indeed.

At precisely 6:42 A.M., the ground beneath the awakening city suddenly started twisting and rocking in a steady east-west motion, accompanied by a sound that one survivor described as like "a million dogs crunching on a bone." The vertical masonry along fourteen blocks of State Street groaned and then began coming apart. Cornices overhanging the sidewalk and parapet walls of brick joined in a common avalanche, flattening parked cars and squashing one unidentified motorist behind the wheel.

In the four-story San Marcos Building, an early-to-work dentist felt his office floor drop beneath his feet and little more, as he plummeted fatally down toward the basement, where the building

46

superintendent was at what would be his final earthly chores. Up State Street a cook was preparing a last breakfast in the restaurant he co-owned with a brother whom he would never see again.

In the four-storied St. Francis Hospital the hollow-tiled walls disintegrated, and a doctor and nurse suffered leg injuries when they leaped out of upper-floor windows to the ground. In Mission Santa Barbara—the city's famous and beloved landmark and a scarred veteran when it came to the destructive force of tremblors —a High Mass was in progress when the violent jolt started the church swaying. As statues began to topple, Father Raphael Vonder Haar, who had been celebrating the Mass, started running from the altar. Just then Brother Michael Lamm grabbed him and pulled him up and away from a large statue that crashed to the sanctuary floor. Some fifteen panicked parishioners broke for the front door, only to be stopped by another priest who warned them from the choirloft that the church towers were crumbling, as indeed they were. Later, groping their way through blinding dust,

Santa Barbara quake of 1925. The Hotel Californian had only been open two weeks before the June 29 tremor collapsed its outer walls, which were poorly fastened to its frame.

The center dome of the posh Hotel Arlington in Santa Barbara came crashing down, killing two distinguished guests, during the June 29, 1925 quake.

both clergy and laity made it safely outside. But one octogenarian lay brother, extricated from a heap of plaster, succumbed nine days later.

The initial shock lasted eighteen seconds, followed fifteen minutes later by a series of briefer aftershocks. But it was the first shake that razed State Street and claimed thirteen lives and injured sixty others. Nor were the casualties exclusively Santa Barbarans about their workday tasks. Then, as now, the city hosted well-heeled visitors seeking rest and relaxation in an Elysian setting. The Californian Hotel, only two weeks completed, had its outer walls shimmy then slowly dissolve and fall, fortunately outward, exposing to the world what could have been an open-fronted Hollywood movie set, complete with occupants in bed, dressing, or at their morning toilette. The rooms and baths were not as private as advertised, but all would live to register whatever complaints they had.

Humor took a holiday from the posh, palatial Hotel Arlington, a popular lighting place "for travelers of two hemispheres." In the words of manager A.L. Rich, the building that he thought was "strong as a fortress" was shaken back and forth as if it were a rag. "One would not believe it possible," he grieved, "for a building to move with such force in so many directions and apparently so limply as did the Arlington. . . . "

What in fact happened was that the Arlington's handsome center dome had come undone and plunged through rooms of distinguished guests. Mrs. Charles Perkins, millionaire widow of a prominent railroad magnate, was rudely buried with her ermine cape and the $200,000 worth of jewelry at her bedside. In a nearby room twenty-four-year-old Bertram B. Hancock, the only son of Los Angeles real estate and oil entrepreneur G. Allen Hancock (himself the recipient of fractured ribs and collarbone and severe contusions), died in his sleep of a broken neck and crushed skull. That out of thirteen random deaths two should have been millionaires defies, of course, all the laws of probability—except, perhaps, in Santa Barbara.

In terms of what could have been, Santa Barbarans had to count themselves lucky. The early hour of the quake saved many who had business downtown later in the morning. Also fortunate was the fact that the first onset of rocking and twisting lasted only eighteen seconds, allowing householders to flee their topsy-turvy homes before the many aftershocks jolted the city—more than 250 of them in the first week. Then, too, Santa Barbara had learned something from San Francisco's mistakes. With the tremor's first slamming impact, Southern California Edison's night operator staggered through a curtain of falling concrete to make sure the electrical current was switched off. His counterpart at the Southern California Gas Company braved the menace of vibrating machinery to close the large valve through which the city received its gas; engineer H.F. Ketz would later be given the proverbial gold watch by the president of the company for his heroism.

These precautions against fire were validated even before the first hammering ceased. All was not well with the city's water supply, and it had to do with more than some busted mains. Four miles upslope in Sycamore Canyon behind a 700-foot crest of fill, Sheffield Reservoir, the secondary source of the city's water supply, suddenly was a reservoir no more. The dam's base was poorly drained and the ground well saturated, and the shock of the quake was all it took. The central half of the barrier pivoted on end and swung open like a door, releasing 40 million gallons of water that swept great boulders oceanward and innundated the lower sections of the city. On higher ground, however, a concrete, arched dam held Gibraltar Reservoir, the city's main water supply, with nary a crack on its face. And in a matter of hours, water from it was sent to stricken Santa Barbara via a bypass.

Whether due to habits of self-discipline or simply to good breeding, Santa Barbara's coolness under fire extended beyond respected civil servants. Ole Hansen, a former mayor of Seattle who no doubt appreciated California sunshine more than most refugees from the North and East, was an impressed observer to that. He couldn't get over how none of the locals got excited when building after building came crashing to earth. The man who fascinated him most was a waterfront street sweeper. Even as the quake was in progress and all hell was breaking loose, the guy kept pushing his broom, not even looking up from his work.

By 9 A.M. volunteer cleanup crews were already removing the rubble of State Street, while American Legionaires and Boy Scouts patroled the avenues to assure order until help arrived. Los Angeles immediately dispatched some of its efficient police to spell them, and in a few days four companies of Marines were on the scene to deter looters. Curiously, there were none, and the whole show of force seemed slightly silly. Santa Barbarans merely settled on their lawns where they boiled coffee, fried bacon, and swapped "where-were-you's" under a golden haze that hung over the city.

Even back in 1925 Santa Barbara enjoyed good press. Papers across the land, but most notably those in New England, Atlanta, and other strongholds of gentility, sent their condolences, sugared with praise for a city loved by all admirers of beauty. Thank God the day's catastrophe had been offset by some good news in the papers: Calvin Coolidge's ailing father had been pronounced out of danger.

Besides lending a police contingent, Los Angelenos opened their pantries and sent food to the stricken city for three weeks. Los Angeles bankers, expressing their "personal and sentimental" interest in Santa Barbara's welfare, opened their hearts by pledging unlimited credit for the rebuilding effort, their generosity tempered, perhaps, by the awareness that in California collateral doesn't come any better than choice seacoast properties.

Most of Santa Barbara's 30,000 citizens patiently waited weeks for the restoration of gas and electrical service, cooking their meals with coal oil. Truly, in courage and in civic virtue they had won high marks. In only one department had they failed.

By happy chance, the eminent geologist Bailey Willis, professor emeritus at Stanford University and president of the American Seismological Society, was a vacationing witness to the June tremor. He was lying awake in his Miramar quarters at 5:42 and at first thought a train was heading toward him from the east, along the Southern Pacific railroad tracks. Following the initial vibrations came a sharp jolt, and immediately he recognized it for what it was, the advancing shock wave of an earthquake. Instantly he was Bailey Willis, trained seismologist, with the opportunity of a lifetime. He calmly counted off the seconds, reaching out a hand to steady himself on the writhing bed which, he noted, was rotating in a counterclockwise direction. When it stopped, he rose and unhurriedly dressed, taking exactly nineteen minutes to do so, ticking off in the interval five distinct aftershocks. Then he went outside to get down to business.

In a matter of days Willis had his conclusions drawn: the disturbance had originated in the west, probably under the Santa Barbara Channel, and ranked as "a local shock of moderate severity."

Of moderate severity? Some Santa Barbarans were put out by this belittling of their disaster. Hadn't the man seen State Street?

Well, yes, he had. And he pulled no punches on that score. What would have passed as "just an interesting experience" became a tragedy because of buildings that were shabby, of poor design, and badly constructed. His remarks were not confined to State Street's eyesores, either. The just-finished California Hotel lost its walls, he said, because they were not properly fastened to the frame. The San Marcos Building, its heavy concrete lightly reinforced, lacked sufficient diagonal bracing for the weight of its walls and arched concrete floor. As for the princely Arlington, he blamed "architectural ambition" for the construction of massive brick towers next to a large open rotunda, across which there was inadequate bracing. "Never trust buildings to mass and rigidity," was Willis's terse overall advice.

Several architectural engineers supported Willis's findings.

51

Though an estimated 85 percent of the city's private homes had been damaged to some degree, most had held up well—particularly the wood-frame homes with cross-braced walls anchored to concrete foundations. It was the public buildings and places of business—well over 300 of them—that were ruined or seriously damaged. Numbered among the total wrecks were five hotels, the two principal hospitals, two banks, four of the largest churches, and four of the largest schools.

The Santa Barbara earthquake awakened some Californians to their common peril, and in the next few years several communities adopted building codes requiring design features that could withstand lateral as well as vertical forces. Unfortunately, those and later codes have not been uniformly applied, or have been evaded. And in any case, they could not be made applicable to unsafe structures already standing. Despite the lessons learned in Santa Barbara in 1925, and elsewhere later, substandard structures— many of them public buildings or with a service function—still exist throughout California as potential deathtraps and headline makers.

The chief beneficiary of the Santa Barbara earthquake was the Community Arts Association. It was not about to let the city repeat the folly of San Francisco, which so thoughtlessly had discarded its Burnham Plan. Before the abundant dust had quite settled, it went into determined action. Pointing to their pride and joy, the newly built Lobero Theatre, which also served as their headquarters and had come through the ordeal with hardly a crack on its stucco face, members spread the message of a rare opportunity. Merchants, property owners, architects, and city fathers huddled and quickly established, by ordinance, an Architectural Review Board. By August 5, one-hundred-two building plans had been passed on, and permits issued.

Santa Barbara was putting on its pretty Spanish face in earnest, to be enhanced by a liberal application of California cosmetics and sunshine.

6

THE QUAKE
THAT CAME TO DINNER

The Friday afternoon's onshore breeze was just reaching Pasadena, where Beno Gutenberg, the renowned geophysicist, strolled the Caltech campus deep in animated conversation with a dear friend and on a subject dear to his heart. Gutenberg's friend was none other than Albert Einstein, the subject was earthquakes, and the Friday was March 10, 1933.

Gutenberg was voicing an old lament to Einstein. Here he was, a man recognized among the world's foremost seismologists, and he had never even felt an earthquake! How he wished that he could, just once. Einstein sympathized, and admitted that he had never felt one either.

At one point their chat was interrupted by John Maxson of the geology department. Maxson came running toward them. "Well, Beno," he said excitedly, "you've finally felt your earthquake!"

Gutenberg stopped and looked at the man, momentarily puzzled. "Oh, no. That's too far away," he responded, recalling a heavy quake that had just been reported in the Tokyo area.

Then the pair turned and walked on toward a meeting with their wives.

Long Beach, California, is a mere fourteen miles south and seaward from Pasadena, as the gull flies. In ways not measured in physical distance, however, it is really closer to Oscaloosa than Pasadena. Its residents are generally a God-fearing lot, compulsive readers and respectors of the Bible, known for the quality of baseball players they produce, for the rich oil deposits beneath their feet and the royalties that got them the *Queen Mary,* and for the down-home hospitality they show visiting sailors of the Pacific

Fleet. In sum, as neighboring Los Angelenos are apt to captiously add it up, Long Beachers are a lot of square bumpkins, so many of them transplanted from the Hawkeye State that their seaside city has been snidely referred to as Iowa's only deep-water port.

Long Beach takes the needling in stride. Its residents count their blessings and their virtues and their oil royalties and they almost always smile. But there were no smiles at 5:54 P.M. on March 10, 1933, when for ten to fifteen seconds they had reason to believe that God himself had jumped right out of the Old Testament on top of them, with two booted feet.

Bernice Brown Blenkinsop, now a happy grandmother six times over, remembers the day as though it were, well, the day before yesterday. She had a lot on her mind that Friday afternoon. Her twenty-fourth birthday was only two days off, and out-of-town relatives were driving in to help her celebrate. Best of all, the celebration was to take place at her favorite mountain place, Lake Arrowhead, among the "tops" of Depression-day Xanadus, where movie actors went to crisscross their Chris-Crafts on the deep blue lake, towing sun-bronzed starlets on water-skis. And just ordinary people, like Bernie, could be a part of the fun.

But that was the *anticipated* weekend, and this was still Friday, and Bernie had other things to do. Namely, to get ready for the evening performance of *Little Women,* in which she, as a member of the Community Players group, played the maid.

The matinee performance had just ended. At half past five, 200-plus appreciative youngsters filed out of the Thomas Jefferson Junior High School Auditorium, while the cast retired to the basement to change, relax and await the seven o'clock, evening curtain. All except Bernie. Instead of joining the rest of the cast, she decided to cross the street to see a friend. So, at 5:54, still wearing her stage wig, Bernie walked out of Thomas Jefferson Junior High.

There was an eerie rumble and the sidewalk seemed to swirl beneath her feet. Across the street, before her eyes, telephone poles started swaying from side to side, the lines alternately sagging then suddenly snapping taut.

"God is with us!" Bernie exclaimed above the rumble which was soon drowned out by the sounds of cracking, splitting, and finally the roar of buildings falling. Behind her, Thomas Jefferson Junior High fell into dusty piles of brick and masonry, trapping the rest of the cast of *Little Women* in the basement. They would

Jefferson Jr. High School was one of the many Long Beach schools that suffered devastation late that Friday afternoon in 1933. The near-calamity led to enactment of the Field Act that made the state a watchdog over school construction.

spend an anxious hour in a successful search for a way out, but Bernie didn't know that. She hadn't even heard the collapse of the school behind her, for by this time she was running—down the street to stop a car, any car, that could drive her home so she could see if her family was all right.

A motorist did stop, and on the drive toward East Second Street, she saw the extent of Long Beach's damage in the California bungalows that had their porch supports bent at precarious angles, and the storefronts that had spilled their glass and wares beyond the curbs.

Bernie was relieved to find her family safe and united, including her brother Roy who had driven into town to see her perform on stage. Roy had stopped his car during the quake because he thought he had a flat tire; that same rippling pavement had caused a couple of other Long Beach motorists to lose control of their cars . . . and their lives. But the danger was not over for Bernie and her family. A panic-promoting rumor, already spreading like an oil fire through the low-lying coastal city, had reached them: a "tidal wave" was on its way!

The "tidal wave," more properly a *tsunami,* was nonexistent, but its alleged coming was as virulent a rumor as the many others that put Long Beach to the test that March night.

Bernie's family hurriedly packed the car in the early evening darkness and joined a swelling exodus. Their own destination was the only high ground close by, fabled Signal Hill studded with resilient wooden oil derricks that had withstood both the vertical and shearing forces of the shake. Beneath the wooden towers that squeaked through the aftershocks, they huddled and spent the night with thousands of townsfolk, feeling secure until they remembered a huge petroleum storage tank on the hill. What if that were to blow? Maybe the best thing to do was just go home.

Below Signal Hill a flight inland continued, in everything from Model A's to Pierce Arrows, drivers helping themselves at abandoned gas pumps where some literally pumped the tea-colored liquid from the cylindrical glass-topped tanks with the chicken wire webbing inside. Mattresses and prized belongings were tied to the flat-topped cars heading east, as if the Okies, the Hawkeyes, and then some, were going home.

There was no tidal wave to legitimize the panic. Captain Augustin T. Beauregard, aboard the flagship of the more than one-hundred vessels of the Navy fleet anchored offshore, knew that. In fact, he was the first outsider to know what had happened in Long Beach. Beauregard put together the sudden watery heave that lifted the giant ships and sent sailors sprawling with the equally sudden extinguishing of city lights that he had seen twinkling through the thickening fog and immediately had this message flashed throughout the fleet: "Long Beach stricken by earthquake. Ships nearest the city send men ashore immediately to render aid."

Aid couldn't be rendered more "immediately" than it was on that chilly March evening. Within two hours, 3,000 Marines and "Blue-jackets" were ashore, manning relief stations in Lincoln Park and patrolling the littered streets. The *U.S.S. Constitution,* "Old Iron-sides" herself, which had tied up at Pier 1 that morning on a good-will tour and welcomed aboard its first gangs of excited school children about noon, was transformed at once into a first aid station. Yes, Captain Beauregard and the U.S. Navy had done themselves proud; the encomiums received from grateful (and "banked") citizens would cover ten years of rowdy shore leaves to come.

Long Beach was especially hard hit by the tremor to which it would give its name. All communication with the outside world, including emergency phone ties, was severed for several hours, as aftershocks rocked the blacked-out city. Business buildings were a

Guarding the rubble . . . The U.S. Navy came ashore immediately after Long Beach was rocked by an earthquake in 1933. The show of force seemed unnecessary as residents went immediately to work rebuilding their city.

shambles, particularly on East Anaheim Street where many bodies lay smashed under fallen walls and cornices. A few fires roared out of control despite the early shutoff of power and gas lines, partly because the Central Fire Station had collapsed and several firemen had been killed or seriously injured. At Seaside Hospital doctors continued surgery by flashlight, only a few feet away from the rubbled walls. They delivered a child, attended to a mastoid infection, then turned their attentions to the quake-maimed and mauled— those who, when rushed in, were still alive.

That night survivors who hadn't left town built bonfires in the gutters and slept under makeshift tents or in their cars, rather than enter their homes that groaned with each successive aftershock. They were well advised. An estimated 2,100 private homes had been damaged beyond safe habitation, a disproportionate number of them wood-frame California bungalows supported on two-and-a-half-foot-tall wooden stilts, or "cripples," placed between sills and basement walls, where the termites had been busy. But the most appalling damage reports would later come from the city's eighty-five schools, which were 75 percent destroyed. Polytechnic High and Jefferson Junior High were the big average-raisers, hideously twisted and pulverized total wrecks that, had the quake struck two hours earlier, would have brought sorrows too painful to think about.

Once the quake dust had settled, the subject of the ruined schools was thought about—thought about long and hard by some very concerned fault-finders. "Architectural effect," read the report of the National Board of Fire Underwriters, "seems to have predominated at the expense of strength, and there was excessive use of ornamentation, towers, heavy copings on thin wall sections, and high parapets." A disturbing feature, the report continued, was the unnecessary structural loadings that were "generally placed over doorways and passageways, with the result that these exits were covered with debris. . . . "

The criticism was taken to heart. In May of 1933, the California Legislature passed the Field Act, which empowered the State Division of Architecture to review and approve public school building plans and specifications, and provided for state supervision of actual construction.

Long Beach, as with San Francisco before it, gave its name to a tragedy that extended far beyond its city limits. Of the total 120 deaths caused by the quake, Long Beach counted only 52. The other fatalities were spread wide, from Los Angeles through Watts down to the Orange County towns, with the heaviest concentration in close-by Compton. That community had also suffered terrible destruction of its buildings, put by insurance underwriters at a whopping 29 percent of total assessed value.

As for the vital statistics of the quake proper, they too told a story that went beyond Long Beach. The temblor's focus was actually 3.5 miles off Newport Beach, five to six miles below the water's surface, on the Inglewood-Newport Fault—a seismic rift that had previously acted up in 1920. The magnitude was a modest 6.3 on the Richter Scale, putting it on a par with the Santa Barbara tremor of 1925. Why then had this "moderately strong local shock," as Harry O. Wood, Research Associate in Seismology at Caltech, described it, wreaked so much more destruction, claimed so many more lives? The verdict of the experts held few surprises. The region affected was densely populated and the buildings poorly constructed. Long Beach and Compton suffered most because they rested on a deep plain of water-soaked alluvium, just the right soil conditions to maximize havoc. Corona del Mar and Laguna Beach were actually much closer to the quake's epicenter

After the quake of 1933: a church in Long Beach with its ironic reference to "The Rock."

and as near to the fault, but the effects there were slight because both were much closer to bedrock.

Long Beach and environs had been hard hit, all right. But where nature stopped, human panic and a less-than-responsible press had taken over. Among the first reports out of the stricken area were that Santa Catalina Island had been swallowed by the sea; that Long Beach had been swept away by a tidal wave; that it had been consumed by fire. By any rumor you wanted to believe, Long Beach was no more. Condolences poured in from around the world, from German President Von Hindenburg and Japan's Emperor Hirohito. And good old footloose and tongue-loose Teddy Roosevelt wired from Manila: "Deeply distressed over tragedy in Southern California. Wish there was something I could do to help."

T.R. may have been helpless, but not so the merchant princes of Southern California who, in the quake's aftermath, resolved to right the record and improve on it some. Boosterism was big

Water-soaked alluvial soil behaved like jelly during the 1933 earthquake, and this San Clemente Spanish-style home literally sank into the earth.

(above and below) San Clemente, May 4, 1933.

in those sunny bygone days on the southern Pacific slope—bigger even than on Main Street or in Gopher Prairie. Bad news was bad for business, which was bad enough in 1933 anyway. Besides, earthquakes simply weren't the bad news everybody tried to make them out. It was time people found that out.

Some Los Angeles Chamber of Commerce flacks claimed the city had come through the quake unscathed, with no damage whatsoever. The powerful Los Angeles *Times,* then in its "America First and Southern California Firster" phase, launched a counterattack on nature and all the sensation-mongers who were slandering the Southland. Shoppers would suffer no inconvenience in Los Angeles, it assured readers the day after the quake. As for the out-of-state offers of assistance, they were dismissed with a terse thanks-but-no-thanks. Southern California was "amply able to care for her own."

What particularly nettled the *Times* were the gory stories going out over the wires with a Los Angeles dateline. One way to combat this, the *Times* suggested, was to mail to distant friends "copies of Los Angeles newspapers."

For days after the quake the *Times* ran stories on how cyclones, tornados, and floods were more to be feared than earthquakes, and authorities were marshaled to make the shaky claim that a properly constructed building would suffer no damage from even the most severe earthquake shocks.

The fulminations reached their peak on March 15 in an editorial titled "The Country Should Know the Truth" and set in 18-point type, which concluded: "The records of fifty years show that no place on earth offers greater security to life, and freedom from the dangers of natural elements, than Southern California. . . ." The same edition gave featured front-page position to a story on tornados that had killed fifteen in the South. This on the day that most newspapers were devoting banner headlines to Franklin Roosevelt's historic reopening of the nation's banks.

In a March 23 editorial the Long Beach *Press-Telegram* also strained to see a silver lining. The city is "safer today than it was prior to March 10," it announced with a reassurance that must have seemed cold comfort to its readers, many of them refugees still living in tents pitched in the city's parks. The *Press-Telegram* went on to urge support of the local Chamber of Commerce in a most worthy effort. As in past quakes, opportunistic hustlers had dusted off their cameras and taken to the streets to focus in on the worst ruins. They clicked away, then quickly put together postcard-size horror books that could be bought and mailed to impress folks "Back East." Well, the local Chamber had done its own selective photography and printed up 200,000 picture postcards that showed the city's "sturdy skyline as it appeared two days after the quake." These could be mailed as printed to worried relatives and friends for as little as a penny and a half, three cents if a written message was "placed thereon." In any case, one had the civic duty of at least writing a personal letter to that aunt or nephew mired in the East, that informed them of the New Long Beach abuilding.

The campaign against nature and a bad press found another champion in Don Lee, the greatest of Southern California's car salesmen, future owner of influential radio station KHJ and (in those days just following the reopening of the banks and Long Beach's closing of its damaged schools) the all-powerful executive secretary of the all-powerful All-Year Club. The Club's aim was to sing the praises of Southern California to those who would come with money in their pockets, either to visit or to stay. Just so the money stayed.

"Good afternoon, ladies and gentlemen," Lee greeted his radio audience on April 4, 1933. His advice about the recent earthquake was to "forget it and let the folks in the East do likewise." Already news of the tremor had been pushed off page one by a tornado in Tennessee, a flood in Ohio, and a cyclone in Louisiana, he reminded his listeners. He also reminded them that tourists were the third largest source of new income for Southern California, spending no less than 700,000 Depression dollars a day. "If you start penalizing a community for having quakes, where are you going to stop?" he wanted to know. Not that he or the All-Year Club was going overboard. The flood gates were not being left wide open for the riffraff. With a hearty second from the Los Angeles *Times,* he wanted the world to know that the unemployed were decidedly not welcome in Southern California and would find no work there.

In the destructive wake of the so-called Long Beach quake, a fact-finding committee was created by the powers that were. The Joint Technical Committee on Earthquake Protection was comprised of physicists, geologists and engineers, and chaired by Robert A. Millikan of Caltech. If those same suited-and-tied powers expected a nice, safe, clean whitewash of the Promised Land from the committee, they got a shock when the findings were

Bread line in public park in Long Beach, a common sight in 1933, as it had been in San Francisco's public parks in 1906.

published in June of 1933. No, the worst was *not* over. Yes, Southern California could expect damaging crust upheavals, and one as lethal as the San Francisco quake of 1906 could occur most anyplace, at most anytime. The committee had strong words for builders and developers who threw up unsafe structures on unstable land. As for those in positions of responsibility who relaxed building codes under political pressure, they were tampering with the lives of children yet unborn.

William A. Simpson, president of the Los Angeles Chamber of Commerce, swallowed his civic pride in his prefatory letter to the committee's report. He couldn't resist taking a slap at the rest of the world and the nation, heir as they were to devastating tornados, floods, hurricanes, storms, and plagues. But he did concede that, in quake-susceptible Southern California, "life and property are subject to hazard in varying degrees, and only by constantly improved measures of protection can those hazards be minimized."

Today's Southern Californians, and northern Californians too, can only wish that those "measures of protection" would have been stronger, less watered down by the conniving of those with land and homes to sell to innocent, later arrivals.

The real heroes and heroines of the Long Beach quake did not

64

get their names in the papers. They were the ones who lived in tents in public parks and were fed from communal soup kitchens, victims first of the Depression, then of dispossession. Their likenesses—faces angular and hollowed with suffering, bodies lank in overalls or long, drab dresses that were surely the very nadir of American fashion—stare out from Brownie snapshots, blurred facsimiles of faces seen in the photographic art of Dorothea Lange. Their words, occasionally repeated by the press, reflect that period-blend of tough sentimentality and gallows wit, echoing dialogue from Steinbeck's novels.

One anonymous wag was quoted as saying that the earthquake was just "another bum shuffle in the New Deal." Another, addressing big neighbor Los Angeles, marveled at how that city could tell the world it had suffered no damage and still put in for a two million dollar reconstruction loan. "They haven't anything to build," went the wry observation, "but they can use the money."

Long Beach's parks remained refugee camps for months following the quake, but the atmosphere was by no means one of gloom. In the best tradition of America-under-stress, its people came together in a spirit of generosity and let's-get-on-with-living. Nightly dances brightened life in the tent cities. Outdoor kitchens fed countless thousands food that wasn't fancy but substantial, and served by many different hands. The Red Cross, which had collected $120,000 in relief funds by March 19, nine days after the quake, was the premier benefactor. The Salvation Army was also on hand, the Elks operated a mess hall for all comers, and the owners of the gambling ship *Monte Carlo* anchored offshore returned some of their roulette and crap-table takings in meat, potatoes, and cabbage dished out at a makeshift Seventh Street kitchen.

Schooling sans schools resumed on April 3. Classes convened under campus trees and in athletic grandstands, away from the buildings that still stood but shivered unsafely through weeks of aftershocks. Librarians also moved their dusty tomes out into the sunlight.

On April 23, President Franklin Delano Roosevelt signed a relief bill authorizing low-interest loans to be channeled through the Reconstruction Finance Corporation. The five million dollars allocated helped, but it was hardly sufficient for all the shattered city—particularly those whose Depression credit was as thin as their wallets. So, many householders enlisted the aid of relatives and neighbors and handyman friends. With borrowed wedges, sledge hammers, jacks, and scavenged lumber, they lifted up and patched together their homes. Slowly, with much pluck and more sweat, Iowa's deep-water port was made whole again. One woman, remembering those hard times many years later, said simply, "We're all of us good common-sense people, and we just took it in stride."

Bernice Brown Blenkinsop never made it to Lake Arrowhead to celebrate her twenty-fourth birthday, though that was the least of the inconveniences caused by the March 10 stirrings along the Inglewood-Newport Fault. Beno Gutenberg, removed more in thought than in miles from the action, fared better—but not right away. When he and Einstein met their wives and admitted they had missed the earthly commotion, they took tongue lashings deserved by two such absent-minded professors. An exasperated Mrs. Einstein turned to Mrs. Gutenberg and sighed, "What a pair of schlemiels we have!"

Later that evening, Gutenberg took his family out to dinner at a Pasadena restaurant. When a particularly sharp afterjolt rattled the china and shimmied the tables, one cool-headed diner arose to calm the nervous patrons.

"You don't have to worry," he announced. "Professor Gutenberg, the noted seismologist, is here. If there were any danger, he wouldn't be out in a public place."

Beno Gutenberg smiled. Schlemiel or not, he had finally felt the earth move.

7

SHIFTING SANDS

"America's Sahara" is an old name given to the southeastern corner of California, the Colorado Desert that lies west of Yuma, Arizona, and the river that gives the 2,000 square miles of one-time wasteland its proper name. Its resemblance to the famed North African desert has since been authenticated by Hollywood's movie makers who have used the sand dunes west of Yuma to put French foreign legionaires through their feats of derring-do, hound the Desert Fox Rommel, and make *The Flight of the Phoenix.*

You might think that so desolate a place would be shunned by man. You would be wrong. Indians in prehistoric times dwelt in the desert's sunken center along the shores of an enormous fresh-water lake—Lake Cahuilla, as it is known to students of the earth. And though Cahuilla dried up before white men ever reached the New World, the southeast corner of California was destined to be the stage for more history than any wasteland would seem to deserve.

That history began early—in 1540 to be exact, long before there was a Jamestown in Virginia, longer still before the Pilgrims put their persecuted feet on Plymouth Rock. The man who wrote the first chapter was Hernando de Alarcón, a Spanish explorer sailing under viceregal orders. Alarcón with his three ships followed the wake of another Spanish mariner who the year before had sailed up the Sea of Cortez and discovered that California was separated from the North American mainland by only a river—and was not an island as everyone had supposed. It was Alarcón's charge to proceed up that river and rendezvous with and supply the land army of Conquistador Franciso Vasquez de Coronado that was marching north out of the civilized comforts of the Valley of Mexico into a harsh and perilous far country. Why? Why were Spaniards plunging a thousand hostile miles into the geographical unknown? Because of reports that the long-sought, fabled Seven Cities of Cíbola were up there, adorned with gold and turquoise that needed liberating.

Alarcón did everything that could be expected of him back in 1540. He reached the head of the Sea of Cortez, the Vermillion Sea, the Gulf of California—as it's variously called. There the skipper quit his ships and had his men tow two smaller boats up the Colorado River. Alarcón found Indians in this land of river, thicket, and sand. Tactful, he befriended them, and soon they replaced Spaniards on the working end of the tow ropes that eventually brought him to present-day Yuma. There he heard from local tribes that "bearded men" like his own were creating a great ruckus east, in the New Mexico of today.

The Colorado's current too swift to go farther, Alarcón stopped and waited for Coronado's army to make the connection. And he waited. Finally he got tired of waiting and floated back down the Colorado and went home. Behind he left a letter that explained his reason for going: worms were eating up his ships.

Alarcón's letter was found later that year by Melchior Diaz, a lieutenant of Coronado who arrived on the Colorado with a column to link up. Diaz and his soldiers were not favorably impressed by what they saw. The "Valley of Torture," they called it.

As inhospitable as the Colorado Desert might have seemed, it was so strategically situated that the Spaniards had to come back. And they did. In 1774 the worthy frontier soldier Juan Bautista de Anza confronted it with the dream of crossing it. Beyond lay the young and suffering province of Spanish California that was certain to die if it could not be supplied by land, from Sonora. With the help of the powerful Yuma Indians, who controled the crucial confluence of the Colorado and Gila rivers, Anza blazed the desert trail to the Pacific. In 1775-1776, as the thirteen colonies prepared to war on England, Anza again crossed and recrossed it, again with the help of the Yuma Indians, but this time escorting colonists bound for Monterey and the settlement he himself would locate: San Francisco.

The brilliant Anza was promoted and moved on to better things as governor of New Mexico. But without his skill and statesmanship the path that led from Sonora to the ocean, described by Spaniards as the *Jornada de la Muerte* (the way of death) or *El Camino del Diablo* (the Devil's highway) was doomed.

68

Arrogant Spaniards who settled among the friendly Yumas treated them badly, and before the Americans won their independence from Great Britain, the proud warrior people who had long owned the Lower Colorado rose in bloody revolt. In the "Yuma Massacre" of 1781 more than one-hundred Spaniards were slaughtered and California's lifeline to Mexico was cut. Cut permanently, as far as the Spaniards were concerned. Their California survived, but in a stunted condition, easy pickings for first Mexico, then the United States when it answered the call to Manifest Destiny in 1846.

Westering Americans followed in the footsteps of westering Spaniards, which had a way of always leading across that damned desert—at least if you wanted to get to the coast of Southern California. Stephen Watts Kearny's conquering Army of the West hoofed across it in 1846. Behind him by two months came the famed Mormon Batallion. A few years later surged a tide of more than ten thousand argonauts who took the southern route to the California gold-fields, by way of Yuma and more than one-hundred miles of desert trail, where they left behind the bones of their beasts and their brothers to bleach in the relentless sun. It was the godawfullest place, this American Sahara. Nothing but greasewood and sage and mesquite when it wasn't just sand. A worthless hell.

Dr. Oliver M. Wozencraft was the one man who disagreed. He had come through with the gold rushers and had kept his eyes and mind open. If you noticed, that Colorado River with all its mad-rushing waters, was a low lying river; and that desert to the west was lower still. All you had to do was tap the river with canals and gravity flow would take water into the parched but potentially productive earth. Doubters hadn't watched the Indians, who worked horticultural wonders with the water of the few springs they had found and used.

Wozencraft, who helped draft California's state constitution, was a spellbinding orator, a skilled politician, and a visionary born before his time. He did manage to get the State of California to go along with his scheme of transforming a hellish inferno into a plowman's paradise. But money to do so had to come from Washington and Congress, before which Wozencraft pleaded his case, off and on, for nearly forty years.

The money that would water Wozencraft's dream to water the desert never came. The Civil War intervened, and the raw and dry Southwest reverted to the control of angry Apaches and opportunistic renegades, as remote from the men who meant to save the Union as the African Sahara.

Wozencraft died at the age of seventy-three, fittingly in Washington where all good lobbyists die, but penniless as most good lobbyists do not. His body was returned to California for burial, but his dream was not interred with him. It was adopted by a Michigan-born engineer named Charles Robinson Rockwood, who also believed the desert could be made to rejoice and blossom as the rose. In time he was to enlist the financial aid of a Yuma doctor, W.T. Heffernan, his friend and fellow visionary to whom the torch had also been passed.

There were years of hard times before Rockwood's California Development Company finally began work, in August of 1900, on a ditch from the river to the desert. Given the land gradient, the canal had first to go into Mexico along the dry bed of the Alamo River before turning north again into the sink of the good old U.S.A. In June of 1901, the first water trickled by way of the Alamo Canal into the thirsty sand at a town to be called Imperial, that would later give its name to a valley.

The early rush of farmers proved premature. The Colorado River, which drains more than 240,000 square miles of the American West, might have been for Indians and Spaniards and Americans alike the river of life. But it was life on the river's own headstrong terms, which some years meant a dwindling trickle, others a silt-laden fury that was somewhere between too thick to drink and too thin to plow. The Spaniards had called it Colorado, or "red," for the color of the iron oxides it carried in thick solution. For Imperial Valley Americans in the spring of 1905, it became the "big red bull" that defied taming.

A heavy snow melt in the Rocky Mountains that year flushed floodwaters more than a thousand miles down its deep chasm, mowing down headgates and sending walls of water to chew up the soft sides of irrigation ditches. Those who created for the Colorado a new channel found themselves powerless to stop its rampage. The farmers tried. They couldn't. Neither could the California Development Company, which collapsed with the walls of its canals. Still the misdirected Colorado roared on, through the wet year of 1906 and into 1907, abetted by the intersecting Gila River that also flooded. Management of the Imperial Valley and the runaway bull now fell to the Southern Pacific Railroad, which had built a spur line to carry to market the first produce. From the eastern office of S.P. President E. H. Harriman came the famous command: "Close the break at all costs."

The Southern Pacific Railroad is cast as a perennial villain in California history. Few would argue that it didn't win the part fair and square. But in 1907 the S.P. donned its good-guy costume and fought the big red bull with all of its considerable resources, emptying trainloads of fill to halt water that was consuming, of all things, a desert! The S.P. won, even though its tracks disappeared under water, its expenditures ran into the millions, and ownership of the valley went back to the farmers anyway. Well, most of it did. Some of it was under water, under the newborn Salton Sea, forty-five miles long and seventeen miles wide, that now occupied the bed of ancient Lake Cahuilla.

Wozencraft and the heirs to his dream were right. Water applied to this desert was a magic potion, and the earth became extravagant even beyond their imagining. The versatile lowland ground raised lettuce, tomatoes, carrots; watermelons, cantaloupes, dates, and figs; peas, cucumbers, cabbage, and squash; oranges, grapefruit, tangerines, sugar beets, honey, and flax seed; wheat, barley, alfalfa, and milo maize—pasturage for cattle, hogs, and sheep. There didn't seem to be anything it could not grow, this fabulous cornucopia, this embarrassment of Canaan. Moreover, with twelve months of growing season under the ever-present sun, fields could be harvested two, even three times a year. Better yet, they could be made to produce the dearest out-of-season crops practically on command.

Of such yields did the Imperial Valley become known as a modern miracle. Imperial also became the name of a new California county that embraced a gaggle of farm towns, including El Centro, Brawley, Holtville, Niland, Calexico, and its sister-city just across the international border, Mexicali. And yet all was not right in the garden—not back in the 1920s anyway. The big, red river that made it all happen still wasn't to be trusted. At times of spring flood it battered the levees and choked the canals with its cargo of silt, keeping men busy repairing and dredging their precious irrigation systems. Then when the river fell in the fall months, Imperial Valley growers faced a danger that stemmed from their own success: a water shortage for the increasing number of fields under cultivation and the resident hands that cultivated them. The bull wanted some more taming. The river needed an equalizing of its flow. Time for another miracle.

The massive Boulder Canyon Project received federal authorization in 1928, and by 1935 the concrete of Hoover Dam was in place, backing the Colorado River's water up into aborning Lake Mead. That was only a part of the project, however. Downstream were planned four more dams and, the apple of every desert-farmer's eye, a brand new canal with power generating stations, bigger and better than anything before. The All American Canal system would run exclusively on United States territory and, with a branch channel some 130 miles long, take Colorado River water north to the neighboring Coachella Valley, another desert about to rejoice.

The All American Canal began continuous operation on September 17, 1940, its silvery fingers spreading west and north, a wonder to behold. But there had been a close call that previous May, on the evening of May 18, to be exact, when the wonder teetered on the brink of becoming a washout. America's Sahara had been shaken to the bottom of its deep sand socks.

Many farm families were doing their Saturday night shopping at 8:37 P.M., when suddenly and unaccountably church bells clanged, burglar alarms vibrated their staccato trill, cars on the road skidded across cracked pavement that shimmied and shuddered. For upwards of ten seconds. Then a pause. The second blow of the combination landed at 8:39. Once more the walls of the valley structures, built in the drab architectural style suggestive of Pocatello and Oklahoma City, reeled and blew out lethal shards of plate glass. Telephone and telegraph lines were down, and the Imperial Valley was temporarily cut off from the outside world—until ham radio operators made contact with one of their own in Laguna Beach.

At 9:54 another powerful aftershock struck with a sullen roar and visited a poignant tragedy on the town of Imperial. Mrs. Wilora Mulling was shopping at Ninth and Imperial Avenue when the shaking started. As her young husband watched helplessly, she grabbed each of her two infant daughters under an arm and ran outside the store—and into tons of falling brick. Juanita Blevins, an eighteen-year-old high school girl saw the woman in her frozen instant of need and reached out for her. Too late. The

Collapsed water towers resulting from the May 18, 1940 Imperial Valley quake added to the fear of drought in this desert-turned-agricultural miracle.

brick struck earth, the woman and her children fatally, and Juanita, who died twenty minutes later in a hospital, in her older brother's arms.

Deaths were few that Saturday night. The quake's force, spent as it was in successive shocks, rather than all at once, kept the count down to nine. Even so, they were widespread, including a young store clerk in El Centro where balconies and arcades meant to shade people from the desert sun came crashing down; young Abel Portillo in Calexico; and a young Chinese who died in a hotel fire across the border in Mexicali.

Below the border the quake did its worst, breaking water mains and igniting fires that couldn't be controlled with half the supply cut off. In a gesture that made F.D.R.'s Good Neighbor Policy more than a gentlemen's windy agreement, three thousand feet of Calexico's fire hose were stretched across the international border to douse Mexicali's flames.

Twenty-five aftershocks were felt before Sunday noon, and by then the fears were mounting. The water . . . what had happened to the canals and the water? First reports were grim. The old Alamo Canal was broken in many places and its spilled waters were racing by the millions of gallons across the deserts of Mexico. The flume of the West Main was destroyed. Lateral canals number 10, 11, and 12 were badly fractured. What about the new all American Canal, the hope of the future, which was just now receiving its first waters? Word was slow to come, though a report that the bridge over the New River on Highway 99 west of Brawley was impassable augured ill. So did the total collapse of the 100,000-gallon water tank at Imperial, the twisted steel wreckage of the tank at Holtville, the damaged water tower at another tanktown, Brawley. America's erstwhile Sahara was suddenly in danger of

This roadway in the Imperial Valley underwent a wrenching displacement during the May 18, 1940 earthquake that measured out at a sobering 7.1 on the Richter Scale.

drying up again, along with the dreams of Wozencraft's children. The immediate fear translated as typhoid fever, since the valley's drinking supply came mostly from the canals, which broken, meant stagnant ponds under the sun's burn, and a possible epidemic. M.J. Dowd, general superintendent and chief engineer of the Imperial Irrigation District, cried for help.

Typhoid vaccine was rushed from Los Angeles, followed by tank cars of drinking water sent by rail. Fifty Highway Patrolmen dispatched to the valley to maintain order were followed by a contingent of WPA workers who wouldn't be leaning on their picks and shovels. With the permission of the Mexican government, three hundred men went south of the border to break their backs at canal-patching. Fortunately, mericifully, thankfully, the All American Canal up north had come through the tremor without major damage . . . just one bad break near Calexico, where the banks had slumped and emptied pond water into the canal bed. The first fears of death by thirst and disease gave way to fears for the next harvest, soon to be shriveling in the cracks of a parched earth that the Spaniards had found. All fears proved unfounded, however. Within six days the canals were mended and the miracle was preserved.

Of all California's big quakes, the Imperial Valley's experience of 1940 remains something of an exception. For some reason, the California Institute of Technology first reported it as rather a mild local disturbance, of less magnitude than the Long Beach quake of 1933. The magnitude was later revised upward to a sobering 7.1 on the Richter Scale. A forty-five-mile tear in the earth's surface ran southeast from just below Brawley to beyond the Mexican border, exposing an unknown fault line that was named the Imperial. Horizontal earth displacements measured out to a maximum of fourteen feet, ten inches, with roads and orchard rows dramatically offset. First estimates of a million dollars damage were also much too low and had to be revised upward to more than six times that amount. Brawley wound up condemning 60 percent of its business district. Imperial and El Centro finished second and third in the loss column.

Killer quakes ordinarily make headline stories in the United States, where natural disasters eclipse human blunders in newsworthiness and sell newspapers for a free press. The Imperial quake didn't. It happened at the wrong place at the wrong time, and did well to get a front-page column anywhere. Only a week

75

before, Hitler had unleashed his blitzkrieg on the western front. By May 18, the Netherlands had gone under, Belgium was in tatters, the French had German armored units within sixty miles of Paris, and the English were in disorderly retreat toward the Channel. Alarmed commentators urged Americans to ready themselves for the Nazi menace. Charles A. Lindbergh advised the nation to ignore the hysteria-mongers and let Europe solve its own problems. History was rendezvousing at Dunkirk, not in America's remote Sahara.

If the Imperial quake held any real surprises, it was perhaps the severity of the tremors, not their location. Seismologists already knew California's desert-southeast as among the state's most seismically active regions, and Imperial County residents get un-

The May 18, 1940 earthquake left its signature on this Imperial Valley orange grove, which shows a shift in its once-perfect alignment of trees.

Crustal rifting and slumping caused by the Imperial Valley quake of 1940. The western reaches continue to pull away from the mainland as the Pacific Plate moves glacially north and west.

happy confirmation of that fact when they buy earthquake insurance and find they are in a high-risk class all by themselves.

The desert rocked many times before 1940 and it has rocked since 1940, and yet the punishing series of blows that landed on May 18 and opened a cut on the desert's face soon engaged more fully the attention of geophysicists. Since then the Imperial Valley has come under their increasingly close scrutiny. In April of 1973 the U.S. Geological Survey and the California Institute of Technology cooperatively installed a network of twenty seismic stations in the Imperial Valley that telemeter data to the Caltech campus. Between June 20 and July 17 of that year the stations were treated to four separate earthquake "swarms"—flurries of smallish quakes that differ from conventional foreshocks in that instead of building up to a big one, they just taper off when they are finished raising insurance premiums. From late January of

1975 into the second week of February, the "net" closed on another swarm, near Brawley.

Monitoring these spates of quakelets (commonly associated with geothermal activity, and the rich Imperial Valley has many potential steam wells) has helped seismologists locate the four major faults that underlie Southern California's desert interior: the Imperial, the Brawley, the Banning-Mission Creek-Sands Hills rift, and the San Jacinto—long considered the most active fault in the whole state. But whatever their separate names, it is now believed they are all related—members of the old and dishonorable San Andreas family, a southern branch. Consult aerial photographs, or just look at a good relief map of California and you will see why geologists think they know where the granddaddy of all California's faults goes after it angles south and east through the state to reach Cajon Pass. Below it dangles a southeast-running chain of depressions and massive earth-slumps. The stretch from the glitter of Palm Springs to the irrigated bottom of the Coachella Valley can be thought of as one link. The way-below-sea-level Salton Sea is another. A slight rise in the land constitutes the Imperial Valley, before the ground builds higher in the Colorado River delta. Then the land drops and vanishes entirely in the blue depths of the Sea of Cortez.

A great division in the earth has created them all. Underneath those rich desert sands that, with water, seem capable of germinating every seed man can plant, the earth is pulling apart, as it has been doing for many millions of years. The results are a steady and continuous fracturing, splintering and rifting beneath the sands of America's Sahara, for which there is no rest.

8

THE WHITE WOLF
AWAKENS

Kern in German means pit, as in cherry or plum pit. Also germ, core, nucleus, nerve center, the heart of the matter. Kern in California is a county, named for Edward Meyer Kern, a Pennsylvania-born botanical artist and topographer who accompanied the illustrious pathfinder John Charles Frémont on his 1845 expedition to California. Such a name for such a place is one of those happy accidents of history, where a good man is honored and remembered, and a borrowed common noun becomes remarkably descriptive. In many ways prosperous Kern County is the core of California, nuclear in being where populous Southern California meets the rest of the state, its nerve center in communications and transportation. The wide-sprawling county also comprises three distinct climatic zones and a wide variety of terrain: classic California hill-and-oak country, a big piece of the Mojave Desert, the forested slopes of the High Sierra, and the agricultural bonanza-land that is the great Central Valley; all that keeps Kern from representing the state in geographical miniature is the lack of a boundary with the Pacific Ocean.

When speaking of earthquakes and earthquake faults, Kern County is definitely at the heart of the matter. Within its border the giant San Andreas veers southeast and into its worrisome bind, intersects first with the active Big Pine Fault that wanders west into the Coast Range, then the great slumbering Garlock that extends east deep into the desert and meets the Sierra Nevada Fault Zone. North of these seismic ganglia, virtually cradled by them, are lesser faults: the Kern Front, the Kern Gorge, the Kern Canyon, the Pleito, and one that had been dozing until late July of 1952, the White Wolf.

July 21, 1952 was a Monday, and the eyes of the nation were on Chicago, where the Democratic National Convention was to be formally opened at 9 A.M. with the crack of a gavel. Delegates breakfasting in the Windy City excitedly discussed the two burning questions soon to be answered: whether Adlai Stevenson would succeed in winning the presidential nomination he was after, and if yes, then would he be able to keep the Democrats of Dixie from bolting the party. Two time zones west, Kern County's farmers and ranchers were beginning to stir at the start of another work week, politics just about, but not quite, the last thing on their minds.

At 4:52 A.M. Aldo Austin, his wife and nine children felt the earth tremble beneath their White Wolf Ranch—then boil and buck and wiggle in every which direction. For nearly a minute there was so much movement they could barely make their way out of the badly wrecked ranch house and count themselves lucky to be alive.

The earth shock sped on. At the mountain-town of Tehachapi, the sides of its homely brick buildings were stripped away by the convulsion, the lights went out, and men, women and children screamed, choked, and moaned as they reached the streets. There they crouched in darkness as water from the town's fallen tank swirled among the ruins. At the nearby Tehachapi Prison for Women, 417 inmates were evacuated without injury from the ruined twenty-year-old structure. Chastened in ways beyond the power of any human penal system, they docilely camped on the prison lawn in tents, without hot water or toilets, and Governor Earl Warren would later recommend that all of them be given a month's credit toward their sentences as a reward for exemplary conduct.

Twenty miles west of Tehachapi, and nearer the White Wolf Ranch, the community of Arvin lost its main-street businesses, save for a hot dog stand. Some 8,000 residents were without electricity, gas, and telephone service.

That was where it started, the so-called Tehachapi tremor of 1952, which in several ways was the most peculiar of California's quakes. It was felt as a long, slow roll, lasting from forty-five seconds to a minute in Southern California, but it was also felt as far away as Santa Rosa in Northern California and in Ensenada, Mexico, far to the south. In magnitude it was major, 7.7 on the Richter Scale, making it the state's second biggest of the century, after the San Francisco quake of 1906. And while deaths were astonishingly few (fourteen, including eleven in Tehachapi) its destructive forces were spent far and wide, and would do more than $160 million in damage. Two water towers toppled in battered Bakersfield, and in faraway Torrance, 50,000 gallons sloshed out of a tank as if in sympathy. Windows were blown out in Santa Barbara; Monrovia's cracked City Hall had to be condemned. The gas main was broken at Castaic, the San Fernando Valley was virtually powerless, and Hollywood had broad fissures in its famous streets. Los Angeles, which had oscillated back and forth an inch in the direction of the epicenter, shed building gingerbread onto its avenues and high tension lines onto its citizens' lawns. (Among the more than ten injured in the City of Angels was a critically burned woman who had tried to sweep a crackling live-wire off her property.)

The superficial damage was random enough. The heavier damage suggested a carefully planned military assault, for hardest hit in Southern California were petroleum installations and transportation facilities. In Long Beach a broken pipe caused an oil refinery to explode and one man was severely burned. In Newhall an oilfield erupted in flames. And at the Paloma Cycling Plant sixteen miles southwest of Bakersfield, the quake collapsed two butane storage tanks and blitzed a transformer bank almost three blocks away. When the volatile gas met the electrical sparks, a tremendous explosion turned the huge plant into a torch that coughed great black billows of smoke over the southern San Joaquin Valley. The six oil companies which co-owned Paloma waged a heroic and successful battle to contain the conflagration, but it was not until four and a half months later, with losses estimated at $1.8 million, that the plant was returned to normal production.

In the Tehachapi Mountains, where the earth shows wounds from tectonic tortures that go far back into geologic time, massive land slides temporarily closed the Ridge Route and cut off stricken Tehachapi and Arvin from Los Angeles. Earthmoving machinery did reopen the road in quick time. But the same did not hold for the rails that switchbacked through the Tehachapis in a series of eight tunnels. There standard-gauge steel rails showed all the rigidity of copper wire when the White Wolf moved. Eleven miles of rail on the western approach to Tehachapi Pass were humped, bowed, S-shaped, suspended over earth slumps, or otherwise in

81

need of replacement. Four train tunnels were shattered, the other four had their linings cracked. In one tunnel a ribbon of steel ran dead into a concrete tunnel wall, yet neither was broken; it was as though the track had been laid and the concrete poured over it.

The Southern Pacific Railroad, operators of the line that transported freight between the two Californias and moved passengers on the "Owl" and the "San Joaquin Daylight," summoned men and machinery from all over the West—from Oregon, Idaho, New Mexico—to work 'round the clock on the emergency repairs. Tunnels Four and Six were "daylighted," Tunnel Three was partially daylighted, and a "shoofly" track was laid around Tunnel Five. Twenty-six days and more than $2.5 million later, the Oakland-Los Angeles service was restored.

From the first zigzags on their seismograms, Caltech's seismologists went after the puzzling Kern County roller. They could not immediately assign it a magnitude or place its epicenter, not exactly. Their first conclusion was that the San Andreas was not responsible. What was then? The Garlock, probably. Then that idea was discarded on the basis of contrary evidence. One characteristic of the Kern County quake was the great number of aftershocks, fifty-three major and ninety-eight minor ones in the first three days alone. On Wednesday a tattoo of three stout ones between 4 and 6 in magnitude shook down the town of Arvin's weakened buildings, but by then mobile units from Caltech's Seismological Laboratory were combing the Tehachapis and closing in on the offender with portable seismographs. The trails led toward Bear Mountain a few miles east of Arvin, and finally to the adjacent, northeast-angling White Wolf Fault, little known, believed asleep.

When the geologists were done analyzing the White Wolf, they had a bundle of surprises. The original point of rupture was ten miles below the surface along a fault that was only traceable for some thirty-four miles—rather small to produce a big 7.7 tremor. As for the actual fault, it dipped steeply at angles from 60 to 66 degrees toward the southeast. The rock on the southeast side moved up relative to the opposite face and slightly to the northeast, making the White Wolf a left-lateral reverse fault with oblique slip movement—a most unusual configuration for California, where severe quakes are almost always caused by right-lateral, strike-slip faults. Nor did the White Wolf move in one simple clean-cut line, but in a complex pattern of cracks and shifts that churned up a fault zone more than a half mile wide in places. Finally, the White Wolf, restless after its centuries of stony sleep, triggered other nearby minor faults into destructive action as aftershocks too numerous to count jostled Kern County throughout the summer of 1952.

One of the aftershocks appended a tragic postscript to the human side of the story in Bakersfield. On August 22, at 3:42 on a Friday afternoon, the core city of California's core county lifted, dropped, and shuddered—for eleven seconds. The dust from downed buildings rose in a great cloud toward the fierce summer sun. Before it settled, two dead were dug from the ruins, the several injured were taken to hospitals, and Bakersfield started counting its property loss: about $49 million for the city proper (Quakersfield, as some locals had taken to calling it) and over $100 million with environs included. Rebuilding began at once.

The punishing August quakelet registered only 5.8 in magnitude, but it was centered close by and made the most of its muscle. Like other minor faults in Kern County, it had been awakened by the White Wolf's howl.

9

THE REMINDER

Lee is in his early forties, a family man once-married, to Jennifer. They have a daughter now ten and a son nine and they live in the San Fernando Valley. Lee remembers having heard a popular song Bing Crosby first sang some thirty years ago extolling the then bucolic, elliptically shaped bowl so worthy of settling in, never more to roam. Lee and Jennifer, and more than 1,200,000 others have since followed the crooner's advice and filled the quondam orchards and farmlands with single-family homes and apartment houses arranged rather haphazardly, at least from a city planner's point of view. Bing, by the way, now lives in northern California, in the decidedly up-scale Peninsula community of Hillsborough, which is only about a mile from the San Andreas Fault.

"The Valley," as it is generally known in Los Angeles, lies mostly within the civic tentacles of L.A., which lies southeast just over the hump of the Santa Monica Mountains. Since World War II the Valley has become a suburban preserve of much of Los Angeles's middle class.

Lee balks at the brand. For himself, he insists on prefacing an "upper" to that Beverly Hills putdown, and cites as irrefutable evidence the most recent tax assessor's statement on the value of his hillside home: $110,000. He will also tell you he is a vice president of a public relations firm that bills over a million a year, and his annual income exceeds $50,000—though he often wonders where it all goes.

Lee thinks of himself as a Californian, and indeed, in appearance he fits the media profile. He is just over six feet tall, still athletically trim and muscular and moves as though his joints were lubricated with Pennzoil. His tan stays year-round from winter skiing at Mammoth and weekly tennis matches at "the club." His brown-tending-to-blond curly hair is razor-cut just a centimeter or two short of fashionable length and crowns a smile that seems permanent, imperishable.

In truth, Lee is not a Californian. Not a native anyway. His parents followed the sun from the Midwest in 1943: his mother was weary of winters that activated her arthritis, his father was after the better wages paid defense workers in California, and both of them were seeking that Turnerian second chance. Lee was only ten then, just along for the ride in the '36 Nash Lafayette that had two flats on Route 66.

As far as Lee is concerned, that does not make him any less a Californian. He did spend his late boyhood and adolescence in the endless sun of Lotus Land, in Glendale, specifically. And when the Korean War broke out and he joined the Air Force to beat the draft, his identity was confirmed in the usual ribbing a Californian takes from the less-blessed troops out of Georgia and New Jersey. "California? Why that's the land of fruits and nuts, where even the weather's queer!"

Lee took it with his usual smile. There wasn't anything nutty about *him*. And as for being queer, his fellow airmen could check his record hustling *josans* during his thirty months of soft duty in Tokyo. That was where he was when the big Kern County quake rang Southern California's bell in 1952. But he did go through two Japanese quakes. Both were sharp tremors, but of short duration, five to ten seconds at most. The first knocked him out of his bunk one night. The other rumbled through Tokyo when he was entwined with a pretty girl on a park bench in the moonlight, and he remembers the whole experience as "almost fun."

Discharged in 1955, Lee came back to California and used Public Law 550 to finance his way through UCLA and take an AB degree. Then it was career time. Public relations. Appearance, self-confidence and a deep store of savvy and energy took him rapidly up the socio-economic ladder, traditionally an easier climb in California than elsewhere. The rise was exhilarating, and Lee made an effort to play out the role of the optimistic, upwardly mobile Southland success story. He dressed well, ate well, and cultivated a taste for California wines. His office on Wilshire Boulevard and the needs of his clients kept him close to the "entertainment world" and the smart people on the Westside. So

he was always on top of L.A.s transitory social trends and stayed
"with it" as long as those trends were safe and not too kinky. On
those infrequent occasions when the subjects of California and
earthquakes were paired in conversation, he had a pat comment.
"You know," he would say, the ever-ready smile masking the little
white lie, "I've lived here all my life and never felt one. Had to go
to Japan for that. Someday I'd really like to go through one here.
Really. Just so I could say I'd been bounced by the homegrown
variety."

Lee met Jennifer on a business trip to Boston in 1962. It was
one of those fine things—they hit it off instantly. In 1963 Lee
married his New England-born bride and brought her home—
rescued her from all that rigidity and uptightness and bedrock
gloom. When they checked out prices of homes in Santa Monica
and West L.A., they decided to go to the less expensive Valley
with its dry autumn Santa Ana winds that made Jennifer nervous,
and tortured her sinuses, and made her long wistfully for the fall
color of deciduous leaves in New Hampshire. But her sometime-
regrets and homesickness were offset by the rambling four-
bedroom Woodland Hills house with its palm-ringed swimming
pool and the sybaritic lifestyle of Southern California.

They went out a lot then and met "important" people "on top
of things." Their politics loosened up, permitting them to put in a
mitigating word or two for Angela Davis, damn the Vietnam War
in its stupid entirety over the second martini, compress their lips
disdainfully whenever Richard Nixon's name was mentioned. They
even sucked a joint now and then—with close friends of course—
after the kids were soundly asleep.

The kids and Jennifer were all soundly asleep when Lee awoke
before the clock radio blared out KGIL's pop reveille on February
9, 1971. The time was 6:01 A.M. and Lee was throwing a foot
over the edge of the California king-size bed when the carpeted
floor came up to meet it. His left ankle buckled but his right foot
quickly braced him atop the squirming concrete slab under the
master bedroom. Instant recognition. "Earthquake," he said coolly
to Jennifer, who was awakened by the bouncing mattress. "Quick,
get in the doorway."

Lee was already under the door-arch that joined to the master
bedroom where each Monday through Friday he always went to
shave, shed his pajamas, and shower, in that order. Jennifer staggered a few short steps to the doorway that led to the hall. She

looked bewildered, scared. Her mouth was open, but she was too stunned to scream.

"Wait it out," Lee said, still cool, arms braced against the trembling portal.

With the words came an acceleration in the shaking. And from the dining room the sound of glass shattering.

The shaking and racket awakened the children who began crying. Then Jennifer screamed and ran down the hall toward their rooms, out from under the protection of the doorway. Lee's nerve caved in too. Ten . . . fifteen . . . twenty seconds had passed. Quakes were supposed to stop before that. He bolted after his wife, turning right into Daisy's room and catching the hysterical five-year-old in his arms, lifting her, holding her against him. In the adjacent room, Jennifer clutched four-year-old Jason and sobbed louder than the child.

Then the rumble became a rattle. Then a faintly perceptible murmur. Then nothing.

Lee gazed across the hall at Jennifer. "Wow!" he said. "That was it! Bet somebody got hurt!"

Jennifer calmed down, or seemed to. But she didn't say much as they toured the house, carrying the still-whimpering children. The eight place settings of Spode china were reduced to two platters, three saucers, no gravy boat. Two shelves of books in the den were strewn across the beige shag rug. But otherwise everything else seemed okay. And the closet door in Jason's room—the one you had to bear down on so hard to even get into—now opened and closed as free as you please.

Since all power had been lost, Lee dressed and breakfasted by candlelight with his transistor radio blaring to get the news, which was sketchy at best. At 7:05 he left for work, without having said much to his wife, who he thought was back on the track, though she wasn't saying much either. Lee took the VW station wagon, leaving the Mercedes for Jennifer. He hoped the freeways were open for his twenty-five-mile commute. They were.

As Lee nosed the VW up the Shoup on-ramp and onto the raised bed of the Ventura Freeway, he jerked his head right and left, peering through the morning sunlight at the Valley's buildings. They looked sound enough. No sign of collapse. His fingers meanwhile worked the radio's tuning knob back and forth across the dial, picking up shreds of information here and there. Yes, it was bad in places. Deaths. The northeastern section of the Valley was a mess. Buildings—big ones—had been leveled. The Golden State Freeway was closed up there; freeway overpasses had come down, blocking the roadway.

When Lee parked his car in the underground garage below the Wilshire District high-rise where he spent his eight-to-six day and hurried over the 200 feet of familiar sidewalk that led to the foyer and its banks of elevators, he noticed shards of thick glass. The Bauhaus tower he worked in had done some shedding. Lucky the quake had hit so early. Naturally, the scare of the thing would be the talk of the office for days.

Jennifer was still in a daze when Lee left. She just couldn't seem to get her thoughts together. Nor could she forget the terrifying noise of the house wrenching in all its joints and the rocks on the sloped roof rattling back and forth trying to obey the laws of gravity. To comfort herself, she lit candles all over the house and decided work was the best thing at times like these. So she threw herself into cleaning the dining room, and was on her knees picking up fragments of china out of the carpet when the first strong aftershock pounded her home. The scream was out before she was upright, this time running out of the house and across the street to her friend Ruth's, where her neighbor first got her settled down and then gave her a stern lecture.

She had done the worst possible thing. "You never," Ruth said, "never run out of a building during an earthquake. That's how people get killed. And for God's sake," she added, "never light candles. The gas lines could break and you could be blasted to kingdom come."

Jennifer has never forgiven Lee for leaving her on the morning of February 9, 1971, and for never having told her about "aftershocks." She'll tell that to close friends over a mid-morning cup of coffee, or during a mid-afternoon bridge game. Secretly, she'll never forgive herself for panicking the way she had, actually running off to Ruth's, leaving the children alone.

Lee and Jennifer came out of the San Fernando earthquake smelling like roses when you put it on a property-loss basis. Much better than Ruth and her husband Ralph, who got an inch-wide crack all the way up their dining room wall and an inch tilt, with cracks, in the slab under their den. This, engineer and native son Ralph explained to Lee, is because his house was on the "fill" side of the hillside street. Lee and Jennifer had lucked out by being on the "cut" side. Lee isn't so sure about that "lucking out." Ralph applied for a federal relief "loan" to mend his losses, and now his dining room and den are good as new, even better than new when you compare the "before" and "after." It almost amounts to a remodeling job; but if you ask Ralph how the transformation came to be, he clams up and smiles, just as wide and open as Lee does when he takes a client to lunch.

At home, however, Lee and Jennifer haven't been smiling much lately. Hardly at all, really. And if you asked them to put a finger on when the trouble began, they'd have to admit it was with the San Fernando earthquake. That was when their lives started to come unglued. Granted, Lee and Jennifer are older now, and Lee will tell you that the seventies aren't the sixties, PR-wise. Some accounts were lost in the recession of '73, and although things are finally getting back to normal, they're not normal enough. There's inflation for one thing. Overhead is up at the office. Not to mention the homefront, where not only are property taxes up, but so is the cost of a standing rib, having the pool cleaned, Jennifer's weekly visits to the hairdresser, and whatever else you want to mention. He'll also tell you, if you're a close enough friend, that he voted for Gerald Ford in 1976. No apologies, either. Everybody has to grow up some time.

Jennifer is a lot more explicit. The crow's-feet of worry have come to "disfigure" (her word) the Celtic face beneath the red hair that increasingly requires the aid of Clairol to hold its color. She simply "wants out"; she has ever since the spring of 1976. There have been all these reports on earthquakes in the Los Angeles *Times* every time you pick it up. Thousands dead in Guatemala. Mangled bodies in Italy. Cities razed in China. Lifeless bodies washed ashore in the backwash of a quake-caused *tsunami* on the island of Mindanao. More than that, there was that man at Caltech who predicted an earthquake for Southern California just as bad as the San Fernando quake of '71. It hasn't happened yet, but who knows? Maybe he knows what he is talking about. She is getting as bad as Lee not reading the Surgeon General's caution on the two packs of Marlboros he smokes every day. She just won't look at the *Times* anymore, except for Jack Smith's column and the rest of the "View" section. Even the magazines they get all seem to sneak something in about "it." Where can you turn? Certainly not to television news—at least not to Dr. George Fischbeck on KABC who tells you to expect, and how to get ready for, "the next big one." How do you face that?

Lee and Jennifer now talk about "her problem" late at night when the kids are abed. He pours the Beefeater while they discuss their marriage and how it can be saved. She is determined to go back to the solid granite of New Hampshire and take the children with her. He is just as adamant about staying put. No imminent wrinkle in the skin of the Promised Land is going to dislodge him from his turf! Besides, he has taken precautions. In the hall closet are two five-gallon jugs of Arrowhead-Puritas water labeled with Magic Marker on adhesive tape, "For Earthquake Only." Right alongside, cushioned from the bottles by pillows, are big cans of Chef-Boy-ar-dee ravioli and Dennison's chili and by-now-stale boxes of soda crackers.

Checking around, Lee has learned that some of his neighbors likewise have water bottles stashed and labeled—some of them relabeled actually, holdovers from bombshelter days of the fifties. As far as Lee is concerned, you may as well just get ready for what may come. If you really belong in the sunshine, you've got to tough it out.

Lee and Jennifer have counterparts in Southern California beyond counting. They are the newcomers, those who have come to build their dreams on land they've been dismayed to learn isn't reliable, isn't steady. Geologists are less subjective; they know the region is seismically active.

Whatever words you want to use, the San Fernando quake was a sobering reminder that the Southland can and does periodically readjust its crust in destructive spasms. Southern Californians, old-timers and recent arrivals, those who had been through tremors before and those for whom February, 1971 was a disturbing revelation, react to such visitations in all manner of ways that have lately engaged the interest of psychologists and psychiatrists. Their speculations are still tentative, but informative.

Most Californians react with an attitude of what professionals call healthy denial. They simply refuse to worry about the "next one." They refuse to see themselves as marked. Now and again, when interviewed on television and informed by reporters who tell them they're living perilously close to an active fault, they shrug, speak laconically. They'll stay put. If it comes, it comes; they'll take their chances. They may know that no earthquake in California, at least to date, has killed more people than die on the state's highways over a typical month. And besides, they see no percentage in worrying about things they can't control. It's a defense mechanism, of course. One that keeps them relatively content and productive.

There is another broad category of Californians, fairly well exemplified by Lee after the shock of '71. Since then even Lee, with his tinned foods and water bottles, has not been himself. He knows he suffers from a vague, generalized tension that might not be so sapping to his energies and peace of mind if it weren't for Jennifer's fears and the consequent strain on their marriage. All the same, even if his family life were just as before, he suspects that the quake pricked worries he never knew he had inside. He doesn't dwell on the "next one" excessively. But he thinks about it enough to make the good life a little less good than before.

Jennifer, on the other hand, belongs with the much smaller number of Californians in whom a sizeable earthquake, or the fear of one, triggers a chronic dread. Often it also releases pent-up guilts that are no less real for being irrational. Some psychologists and psychiatrists theorize that the victim feels he or she is somehow responsible for the awful disruption. They also believe that earthquakes pose qualitatively different stresses on the human mind. Unlike tornados or hurricanes or floods, they strike totally without warning, leaving the victims with feelings of utter impotence. Moreover, they excite one of man's few innate fears, that of falling.

While the San Fernando temblor was for Southern Californians at large a great reminder, it was for earth scientists the great teacher. Never before had so many specialists descended on a quakesite so quickly with so many tools to measure the slackening pulse of the earth or to study the just-ruined ruins in the northeast Valley. Some of what they learned confirmed what they already knew. Some was brand new and instructive, and not a little surprising.

The quake waved out at 6.6 on the Richter Scale, making the actual earth movement slightly more severe than in either the Santa Barbara or Long Beach jolts. Conversely, compared to the forces unleashed on San Francisco in 1906 or Owens Valley in 1872, or the Los Angeles area in 1857, it was no more than a friendly nudge. To put it differently, and not very comfortingly, the maximum possible earthquake that could hit either Los Angeles or San Francisco would be a *thousand times* more powerful in terms of energy released than the San Fernando quake.

The 1971 tremor has been classified as merely "moderate." Southern California experiences one that size every four years. But the San Fernando event differed from most of its equals in that its epicenter (the spot on the earth's surface directly above the actual *initial* point of rupture) was close to a densely populated metropolitan area, and it didn't waste its fury on the sparsely populated desert terrain. Even apart from what the seismographs showed, however, it had destructive properties peculiar to itself that seemed excessive for its size. It was felt over 80,000 square miles, as far away as the Yosemite Valley, Las Vegas, Nevada, even in Mexico, and it left its mark at seismic stations all over the world. Curiously, the speed of its shock waves racing through the earth, as measured on Los Angeles area accellographs, were the fastest ever recorded to that date.

For a moderate-size tremor, the San Fernando shake packed a powerful wallop borne out by the grim statistics: 64 dead, an estimated 2,400 injured, over $500 million in property destroyed. Much of the loss was attributable to human ignorance or carelessness, and that figures weren't higher was attributable not to foresight and wise planning, but to plain old good luck. Again, as has been the case in so many California quakes, the timing saved many and much. Had the earth trembled at 8 A.M., or noon, or 5 P.M., the human misery would have been multiplied. Had it lasted only seconds longer, say the experts (and they say that the "strong motion" lasted only twelve seconds, though those who agonized through it know there was motion of some kind anywhere from twenty seconds to a full minute), the tragedy would have really escalated. The main focus of the duration conjecture is the Van Norman Reservoir complex in the north Valley area, which held back the waters brought by aqueduct from the Owens Valley, no less than 80 percent of Los Angeles' water supply. The water in the lower Van Norman Lake, the major body in the system, fortunately happened to be filled to only a little over half its capacity at the time the quake hit, and no spill occurred when the earth-fill dam sloughed its crest and broken concrete facing into the surging water. The upper Van Norman Reservoir, however, was filled to the brim, and the quake's impact caused the dam to slump three feet and lurch downstream as much as five feet at its crest. According to Professor H. Bolton Seed of UC Berkeley,

*A freeway in pieces . . . The 1971 **San Fernando** earthquake knocked down five freeway overpasses and damaged others that had to be razed on **Inter-**state 5 at the north end of the San Fernando Valley.*

only seconds more of agitation, or if the upper dam had released its water into the lower lake, and there would almost certainly have been a complete failure of the lower dam. And then? A torrent of 8.3 billion gallons of water would have swept through the homes and businesses of 80,000 people, drowning tens of thousands. (Those 80,000 were evacuated from their homes for several days while worried engineers lowered the water level in the reservoirs.) As for property loss, that could have kept a battalion of accountants busy at their calculators for many morbid months.

Ifs became actualities for the State Division of Highways. The quake tore apart sizeable stretches of concrete highway, knocked down five freeway overpasses, and damaged others so badly they had to be razed. Once again, the timing was in man's favor. Two hours later and the carnage would have been a ghoul's guess. Even at the early hour of six, the collapse of one overpass provided the most gruesome chapter in the San Fernando story. Two men in a pickup truck were passing directly under the overpass when tons of falling concrete met the freeway. The passenger compartment was telescoped to a height of twelve inches; a Highway Patrolman noted "a small portion of blood and flesh" protruding from the rear of the right door.

The failure of the spans to stand up to the quake were attributed to an overall failure to design for earthquake forces, and the tie bars that ringed the vertical reinforcing bars in the supporting columns were not of adequate size or spacing to hold under the strain. The State Division of Highways immediately doubled specifications, and in March 1972, millions of dollars were authorized for strengthening existing bridges and overpasses in quake-prone zones.

The San Fernando quake pounded more familiar lessons into the heads of slow-to-learn Californians. Again, public and service facilities were more vulnerable than the common wood-frame family home. Large portions of Los Angeles were blacked out, and some 630,000 customers experienced power outages when the flow of juice from four steamplants and three hydroelectric plants was interrupted. Switching and converter stations suffered severe damage in and around the north Valley, and the supply of power was not completely back to normal for a day and a half. Four gas transmission lines had to be shut off when the upheaval left multiple breaks in the welded steel pipes. Telephone service, under heavy demand by the rash of post-quake calls, was further

hampered by the knockout of General Telephone's Sylmar Central Office, where a hundred tons of switching equipment valued at $4.5 million were demolished.

Sylmar above all other communities was marked for grief, and in Sylmar was laid bare California's greatest shame. There were no lack of warning precedents: in San Francisco, in Santa Barbara, in Long Beach, hospitals—facilities that common sense says are least dispensible in an emergency and harbor the most defenseless— had been ravaged. And Sylmar, if you had to give the northeastern Valley community a descriptive label, was a hospital town. Forty-seven died in the fall of the non-earthquake-resistant Veterans Hospital. At Olive View Hospital two died when power failure shut off their respirators and two others succumbed to quake-caused injuries. That the more than 500 remaining patients and staff got out, or were gotten out of the less than year-old hospital alive was again due to the fact that the shaking stopped when it did. Another five seconds of strong motion would have filled the morgues. Within a few miles' radius of Olive View, Pacoima Memorial Lutheran Hospital experienced major structural damage, Holy Cross Hospital, the Foothill Medical Center, and the Indian Hills Medical Center suffered significant damage.

California seems fated to learn all its construction lessons the hard way, despite the repeated warnings of many engineers and geophysicists. Local governments tend to jealously guard their prerogatives of adopting building codes and enforcing them. That these codes sometimes are slackly enforced, or bent under the pressure of real estate developers and building material suppliers, is a fact of commercial life.

Yet the problem goes beyond just foot-dragging, corner-cutting and favor-doing. The philosophy of California earthquake codes, as spelled out by the Structural Engineers Association of California (SEAOC), has three aims: To build structures that will (1) resist minor earthquakes without damage, (2) resist moderate earthquakes without structural, but with some non-structural, damage, and (3) resist major earthquakes of the intensity of the strongest experienced in California without collapse, but with some structural as well as non-structural damage.

That's put straightforwardly enough, and laudable. But how do you reach those goals? The best teacher is experience, and earth-quakes don't happen every day, and comparatively speaking, are rather infrequent in areas that are built on. And what do you do when you design for one earthquake experience and discover that the next tremor behaves in quite a different way? For example, lateral stress coefficients of 20 percent of gravity were thought safe for a moderate earthquake. Yet the San Fernando tremor released shear forces of up to 1.25 G in the northeastern Valley! How could anyone stay economically competitive and still build a structure that would resist any force that nature could throw at it?

There aren't enough answers. By the same token, not too many years ago there weren't any at all. Today we do know a great deal about what happened in the San Gabriel Mountains on February 9, 1971. The San Andreas Fault that runs a nearby zig in its zigzag course through the state was blameless. The guilty fracture turned out to be the San Fernando Fault, slicing up and northward from under the San Gabriel Mountains at an angle of about 45 degrees. Until that February morning, it wasn't known as a bad actor, its last significant move a gentle one in 1893, when it made its presence known to a handful of Valley farmers and tipped over an adobe in Newhall.

The 1971 earthquake was of the thrust type. That is, a portion of the San Gabriels leaped higher as the plain that Los Angeles reclines on pushed north with compressive forces that are backed up all the way to the toe of Baja California. The flatter lands to the south dove under the range and pushed it up. This game of terrestrial push-and-shove is by no means new. It goes back more than five million years and actually helped to make the San Gabriel Mountains, before there were men around to match even molehills.

To further quantify the villain, the quake's hypocenter (the subsurface point of original rupture) was approximately eight miles under the surface of the earth. There the point end of a wedge-shaped block of deep-down crystalline rock sliced under the mountains and jacked up some 2,500 cubic kilometers of other rock. The undercut earth then jerked up and slid slightly to the west, the total displacement being about six feet, equally divided between vertical and horizontal movement. The surface of the earth split open just south of Sylmar, which was unfortunately on top of the small chunk on the "up" elevator. Similar things have happened before. They will happen again—possibly even before this stripped-down simplification of what was a complex seismic event appears in print.

How do we come by all this specific knowledge? Why do we have a more complete picture of the San Fernando convulsion than any other California quake? The answer is a fascinating and sanguine story of man's long attempt to cope with the most awesome, lethal and bewildering of natural calamities. And the story may yet have a happy ending.

10

QUESTIONS . . . AND
A TRICKLE OF ANSWERS

Why earthquakes? To say that they are caused by movements in the earth is to apply tautological torture to the question. What, then, causes the earth to move?

Though Aristotle gave an early explanation that quakes were due to restless winds trapped in the innards of the earth seeking release, later men became more interested in the "whys" of the dreadful events, not the "how." The Roman Emperor Justinian forbade blasphemy and certain sexual practices to prevent these scourges of God. After him, others likewise religiously inclined viewed the temblors as expressions of divine displeasure and urged their neighbors to mend their ways.

With the dawn of modern science in the seventeenth century the problem was approached differently. God might be the ultimate cause of earthquakes, but He, She, or It by nature must act in rational, physical ways. Ways that could be measured and described.

But the geniuses of science who followed Sir Francis Bacon and René Descartes put their brilliance to work on what was above them and around them, not what was beneath their feet. The earth was solid, after all. And men stood on the very outer crust of that giant sphere. How could anyone get inside and measure or observe anything? Understandably, geology as a science lagged behind other more glamorous disciplines.

For a while learned men believed that earthquakes were the result of vulcanism. Erupting volcanoes often shook the ground as they spewed up molten lava. But then again, sometimes they didn't. More troublesome, earthquakes frequently occurred without any fiery fountains or belches of ash. Well, perhaps the molten matter had started up and been blocked off by rocks that wouldn't budge, and made its presence known in the sudden spasms that toppled cities and changed the features of the land. Aristotle's intestinal gas had become a thick liquid, still seeking release.

Real progress came in the nineteenth century when students of the earth more or less abandoned sweeping theories that described all—in favor of limited observations supported by experimentation. The big picture was shattered into a jigsaw puzzle, with many sleuths at work on piecemeal solutions that, when patiently assembled, might reveal the old mystery and thereby diminish its capacity for terror.

The Irish engineer Robert Mallet was a man fascinated by earthquakes. In 1859, in Calabria, Italy, where a quake had struck two years before, he set off explosive charges in the ground and then timed the arrivals of surface vibrations that made waves in a bowl of mercury located some distance away. Mallet proved man could make his own "earthquakes," that they could originate in the earth's crust rather than way down deep, and that the speed of the shock waves produced could be measured in at least a rough way.

The early work of Mallet was built on later in the nineteenth century, notably by John Milne, an English professor of geology suitably posted in Japan, where earthquakes are many and strong. He, too, manufactured his own tremors by releasing a hoisted heavy iron ball to earth and recording vibrations with a homemade device—a stylus attached to a pendulum that scratched its movements on a smoked glass plate. Milne's instrument was not the first to monitor earth tremors; the Chinese in the second century A.D. had an elaborate and ornate vessel that roughly determined the direction of distant quakes using the action of a pendulum. But Milne was describing quiverings in the earth, both back and forth and side to side. *Seisms*—the Greek word for shakes—were actually being recorded, and seismology, the study of those shakes, had a father. Milne continued to improve on his instrument, devising the means of using photographic paper on which to record shakes and to have that paper continuously moving and printed upon by a clock. For the rest of his life, Milne promoted the establishment of seismographic stations throughout the world.

After Milne, seismographs—"shake writing" machines—were developed in a bewildering variety with all manner of refinements. Many still rely on the principle of the pendulum—a suspended mass that tries to remain at rest when its earthly support moves, the pendulum's meanderings transferred by mirrored light to photo-sensitive paper on a revolving drum. But there are also strain seismographs, instruments set in bedrock that record the stretching and crushing of rock as seismic waves course through. Today's machines may employ electronic magnification and magnetic control, one being tailored to record strong motions in the earth, another sensitive to very slight tremors called microseisms. The modern seismic station boasts an array of specialized instruments that simultaneously record horizontal and vertical earth movements and the acceleration of shock waves.

Seismographs were a boon to seismologists of the early twentieth century. Their zigzag lines of ink that showed up after an earthquake told a story that was at once simple and complicated and crucial to man's understanding of his old enemy. Shifting in the earth's crust released waves that traveled away from the source of the disturbance and left their marks on distant seismographs. Marks, not mark. For what showed up were different kinds of waves which, fortunately, arrived at different times and left in their passing separate signatures.

The first arrivals at seismographic stations were the Primary, or P, waves. They were longitudinal or pressure waves, with a push-pull action. As in sound waves, a particle of matter is struck and knocked forward to knock its neighbor, both to bounce back, but to be a part of a chain reaction that races through the earth in all directions from the place of original disturbance.

Behind the P wave came the slower Secondary wave, the S wave, which conveniently initials its own action, that of shearing, the particles of the earth jarred at right angles to the wave path, moving in the snakelike fashion of a guitar string strummed. It, too, moved at its slower rate through the body of the earth, behind the P waves, but with peculiarities that would eventually inform geologists on the makeup of the earth's core.

Other waves were also identified. Slower still to show themselves on seismographs were the L or "longus" waves, so called for their long wavelengths; these were surface waves that did not penetrate into the earth's interior but were usually of considerable amplitude and were damage-doers. The first of these to arrive were the Love waves (named for their discoverer, A.E.H. Love) that traveled over the earth's periphery in much the same way that the S, or shear waves, do. Finally, there came the Rayleigh waves, after the

English lord who first developed the theory of surface waves; they are slow-moving longitudinal or vertical waves that travel the earth's surface away from a shake, dying out as they go, with a little curl-back kink at their crests.

In the print-out of waves was the first key to the many doors that closeted the earth's secrets; not initially for understanding the mechanisms of earthquakes, but in deducing the composition of the inner earth itself. Geology's stepchild, seismology, was prepared to do its parent many kind turns.

In 1909 a Serbian named Andrija Mohorovicic made a study of seismic recordings following a quake that had rocked nearby Croatia. What struck him as odd was that the P waves, for which a travel time was known, suddenly picked up speed far from their source and reached distant stations faster than they should have. This, he reasoned, meant that the earth's composition changed at some point below the surface as the P waves moved into denser, more conductive matter. This subterranean boundary became known as the Mohorovicic Discontinuity, or "Moho." As more information was gathered it became clear that the Moho separated the lighter sedimentary, igneous and metamorphic rock of the earth's crust from quite different matter below. And that the crust was, in relation to the earth as a whole, thinner than the skin on a grapefruit.

What, then, was "below?"

Again, seismic waves triggered by earthquakes would shed light on the matter. Beno Gutenberg, a brilliant young German scientist who was later to become the senior geophysicist at the California Institute of Technology, saw that light in 1913. Those Primary waves traveling toward the earth's center behaved in a curious way. If the earth below the crust were of uniform makeup, those P waves should just gradually weaken the deeper they went. But they didn't. At a specific depth that Gutenberg calculated, those waves did funny things. Some were reflected back to the surface strong and clear about a quarter of the way around the world from where they started. Others were refracted, or bent, and made it through the heart of the earth—but on an altered course. Most significantly, between 103 degrees and 145 degrees from the focus of the earthquake there were two "shadow zones" through which no P waves seemed to pass at all. The Gutenberg Discontinuity, as it came to be called, became a dividing line within the earth, separating the interior mantle from the much denser core, which was responsible for bouncing back or bending or drastically weakening those P waves.

What makes up that core? Geologists believe it is partly liquid iron and nickel under great heat and pressure, and as evidence they can cite those slower-moving tag-alongs to P waves, the Secondary or S waves. They follow P waves to the Gutenberg Discontinuity and then stop in their transverse tracks. It is a property of S waves that they can not snake their way through a liquid.

Largely through the study of seismic waves, geophysicists have now constructed a fairly detailed model of what the earth is all about inside. If the planet were sliced in two, one could see concentric circles. First, from the outside, there is the rigid lithosphere, averaging about 25 miles in thickness, which includes the cool, light rocks of the crust and a small portion of the mantle. Next is the mantle proper, extending almost 2,900 kilometers towards the earth's center, comprising half of the earth's radius, 83 percent of its volume and two-thirds of its mass. But the mantle itself has two layers. The upper section, about 150 kilometers thick and sometimes referred to as the asthenosphere, is an unstable zone that behaves as an elastic solid; that may sound like a contradiction in terms, but it might be likened to hot iron in a pliant state on a blacksmith's forge. Farther down is the thick, lower mantle, denser and more stable. Finally there is the super-hot core, which also has two layers: the fluid outer core, and the remote inner core which may be fluid also.

As far as the genesis of earthquakes go, it is presently thought that the interactions between the lithosphere and the asthenosphere are critical. But that's now, and that's to leap far ahead in this detective story.

Seismologists in the first decades of the twentieth century found themselves learning more about the earth than about earthquakes. And yet the same P and S waves that coursed through the bowels of the earth also reached its surface, where seismographs recorded them. Early on, seismologists used the data at least to locate the origin of tremors. The method was relatively simple, even if deciphering the seismographic squiggles was not always so. P waves traveled at known speeds and the S waves that followed traveled at known speeds. So it was possible, by taking the difference in their arrival times at a given station, to compute the distance they had come. If three or more stations recorded the waves and made the proper computations, arcs representing distance could be drawn through the three dimensions of the globe. Where the three or more lines intersected was the hypocenter of the quake, the subsurface point of rupture where it all began. As the deciphering of the seismographic records was perfected and more and more stations rapidly exchanged their data, seismologists were able to inform a nation that it had suffered an earthquake even before word of the same filtered in from its hinterlands.

Locating an earthquake was one thing. Quantifying its strength was another. And though those same jagged lines recorded on seismographs told a story of power as well as place, the human need to categorize and classify tremors predated the instrumentation to measure them physically. Consequently, the word "intensity" was more or less usurped by those who described earthquakes in terms of how humans experienced them rather than how machines recorded them.

Out of a host of localized attempts to grade earthquakes in the nineteenth century, a joint Italian-Swiss effort known as the Rossi-Forel Scale became widely accepted, only to be superceded by the Mercalli Scale, and ultimately the Modified Mercalli Scale that is still in use today. The common denominator of them all was that they relied on human experience and observation of an earthquake's destructive effects. For instance, at Step II of the twelve on the Modified Mercalli Scale, the shake is felt by a few persons resting on the upper floors of buildings, and delicately suspended objects may swing. At Step VI on the scale, everyone feels the quake and many run outdoors in a panic; some heavy furniture is moved about, some plaster and chimneys fall, though overall damage is slight. At Step X some sound wooden structures are leveled, the ground cracks badly and some building foundations are destroyed; rivers jump their banks and landslides are numerous. At the maximum XII, damage is total and waves are said to be seen moving across the earth and objects are thrown into the air.

The Modified Mercalli Scale is useful in assessing an earthquake's destructiveness and in mapping isoseisms—lines of equal shaking—that radiate from a quake's epicenter. These do not show the perfect circle configuration one sees when a rock is thrown into a still pond. Instead, they are apt to assume an irregular, elliptical shape rippling away from an earthquake fault, the tracery of the lines often indicating a pattern of equal instability in the affected soil.

But the Modified Mercalli Scale remains a somewhat subjective measure, relying on human senses and a human presence. What about those quakes that wrench the earth where no humans are around to feel and observe? Or where people are few and live in tents and have no masonry structures that would make the intensity scale applicable?

Clearly, there had to be another yardstick. There was. Caltech's Dr. Charles Richter, with the assistance of his colleague Beno Gutenberg, devised in the 1930s the famous scale that now bears the former's name. Since its inception, and with its widespread application, the Richter Scale has been a source of endless confusion and misunderstanding in the public mind.

There is more than one reason for this, and clearing it up involves a series of clarifications. First, it should be remembered that the word "intensity" was claimed first by the Rossi-Forel and the Mercalli scales. So Richter chose *magnitude* to best express the size of an earthquake, on a numerical scale ranging from the relative quietude of Zero to what has been thought the maximum possible wrenching the earth can deliver at Nine. What determines the magnitude is the amplitude (or size) of the seismic waves as recorded by a seismometer. Moreover, in devising the scale, Richter used a specific seismometer, the Wood-Anderson torsion seismometer, with the actual lines on the seismogram to be adjusted for purposes of comparison to how they would appear if the instrument were 100 kilometers away from the earthquake's epicenter.

The scale itself is logarithmic rather than arithmetical. That means each whole-number increase represents a ten-fold jump in amplitude, or ground displacement. Therefore a reading of 6.0—the beginning of the "moderate" spread on the earthquake scale—is not just a little bit bigger than a 5.0; it is ten times greater in magnitude. By the same token, a 7.0 reading (the bottom of the "major" earthquake range) is 100 times bigger than a 5.0. And an 8.0, the base of the "giant" quake range (the convulsions of Fort Tejón, the Owens Valley and San Francisco in 1906 are all believed to have topped that magnitude) is 1000 times greater than a 5.0!

Unfortunately, the opportunities of getting it all muddled do not end there. Earthquakes are also described in terms of the energy they release. There is a relationship between magnitude (as computed from the height of those jagged lines on seismograms)

107

and rampant energy released—probably the most meaningful index of all in comparing earthquakes. But with energy the increase between whole numbers on the Richter Scale jumps dramatically to a factor of anywhere between 30 to 60 times, depending on what particular formula is used to convert from ground displacement to energy. But just say, for the sake of illustration, that it is 50 times. That would make a 6.5 quake (roughly the size of the San Fernando tremor) 50 times more "powerful" than a 5.5. A 7.5 quake (less than the magnitude of the Kern County shock of 1952) would be 2,500 times more "powerful" than a 5.5. And an 8.5 magnitude—sometimes said to be the "Maximum Credible Earthquake" (MCE) that California could experience—would be 125,000 times greater in amount of energy released.

The numbers become dizzying if not incomprehensible. Two things should be kept in mind, however, whenever Richter Scale readings are cited: one whole number jump obviously stands for an enormous increase in a quake's wallop; and the number is not an absolute guide to the quake's properties. Different seismometers can and do record different magnitudes for the same tremor. The amount of ground displacement on one side of a fault can differ from what is recorded on the other. The frequency of the ground waves and the local makeup of the earth they pass through have much to do with how destructive a given quake will be. Also, one quake may reach a 6.0 magnitude by virtue of a single spasm, while another of the same magnitude may produce three of approximately the same size. In short, a Richter Scale number is an imperfect description of what any one earthquake is like. At the same time, it is the best way of comparing quakes that anyone has come up with yet.

The old saying that seeing is believing has a special relevance in science. Belief begins with observation, the weighing of evidence the eye can see. After Robert Mallet, who with his gunpowder blasts made waves in Italy's boot, seismologists with their seismographs went far in visualizing what went on inside an earth that was becoming less and less opaque. By the mid-twentieth century a lot was known about the subcrustal world. Earthquakes could be located, measured, and described in many ways. But one question, the ultimate question, still went begging for a satisfactory answer: what really causes the earth to move?

11

A BREAK
IN CALIFORNIA

Earthquakes can and do occur most everywhere. But serious students of "seismic events" have learned that more than three-quarters of all earthquake energy—at least in recent times—is vented along what is rather misleadingly called the Pacific Rim of Fire. This band of unstable land takes the shape of a giant bent horseshoe, running up from Chile and Peru, through Central America, Mexico and California. Then the bend is west to Alaska, arcing the Pacific and descending along the Kamchatka Peninsula and Japan, only to crumple inward as it runs through the Philippines, New Guinea and on to New Zealand. Here, along this Circum-Pacific Belt, some of the greatest of natural catastrophes have befallen man, including, in this century, the infamous Kwanto quake of 1923 that killed more than 100,000 Japanese and burned more than 300,000 structures in Tokyo and Yokohama, and the 1970 battering of northern Peru that took an estimated 68,000 lives. Also right "on line" is the City by the Golden Gate, reduced to smoking ruin in 1906. Although the loss of life was modest by Pacific Rim standards, the 1906 quake was in many ways the most significant of all. At least in advancing man's knowledge of the forces at work in his trembling planet.

The San Francisco quake was the first to be studied intensively by scientists. It had left behind 270 miles of tear in California's skin and other visible changes that would lead to a remarkable discovery. The San Francisco Bay area had twice been surveyed by triangulation in the nineteenth century, and was again immediately after the earthquake. When the results were compared it was found that the orientation points had moved! And that could only mean the earth moved! And indeed it had—horizontally—

right along the San Andreas Fault. Land west of the rift had lurched to the northwest and that to the east in a southerly direction, showing a lateral displacement of up to twenty-one feet.

This was grist for the seismologists' mill—a phenomenon begging to be explained. Harry Fielding Reid, an engineer with the California State Earthquake Investigating Commission, did just that in 1911. He postulated the theory of elastic rebound. Rock formations attempting to move opposite ways on the two sides of the split had been pressing against each other for a long time, building up enormous forces that finally pushed the distorted mass beyond its breaking point. In a sudden shearing action, the bond was broken and the facing rock "walls" slipped into a state of temporarily relaxed tension.

Reid assigned the blame for earthquakes to faults in the earth's crust. This was discounted by some Japanese seismologists who maintained that these rifts were the results of earthquakes, not their cause. For a while the tiff seemed akin to a chicken-or-egg argument, but some fifty years after Reid described elastic rebound, an exciting new theory would put its considerable weight behind him.

Sciences rarely leap fifty years forward, however. Mostly it is a case of one step at a time, the slow accumulation of minor operational facts, the development of measuring tools and a nomenclature, a continuing exercise in classifying and reclassifying. After San Francisco, the San Andreas was labeled a transcurrent, or strike-slip fault—one in which displacements in the earth are sideways, not vertical. (Its opposite is dip-slip faulting where the earth movements are vertical, though many quakes are characterized by both vertical and horizontal displacements. In the San Fernando quake, for example, movement was almost equally divided between the two.) The San Andreas Fault is also referred to as a "right lateral fault"; that is, if you stood facing it, the land across the fracture would, when it broke free, always move to your right. Finally, the San Francisco quake was of "shallow focus," as all California quakes are, the center of the disturbance being never more than forty kilometers deep, and usually a lot less. These contrasted in significant ways with the deep-focus quakes that commonly occur in deep suboceanic trenches. Deep-focus shocks are generally of lesser magnitude and are not followed by many aftershocks.

About those aftershocks: how could Reid's theory of elastic re-

The granddaddy of California's faults, the San Andreas, central section, where tectonic plates meet, collide, and cause earthquakes.

bound account for them? Was it that the main shock released only the pent-up energy in a particular stretch along a fault, and other adjacent sections had to play a grinding game of catch-up? Or did that first headlong rush of release go too far, so that the rock was in a new bind and had to back off a little to relax?

Answers have a habit of breeding more questions, and one of the most tantalizing to surface after Reid's work was why the earth moved where it did and not elsewhere. The shearing rupture exposed itself from land's end at the Mendocino Coast in the north all the way to San Juan Bautista. But not to the south of that old mission town. And yet the San Andreas Fault ran that way . . . ran a long way that way; down through Hollister and behind the Coastal Range, to the communities of Parkfield and Cholame, south to the dry Carrizo Plain and the barren southwestern corner of California's great Central Valley. There it made a jog to the east and traveled along the transverse ranges that border Los Angeles on the north, only to turn south again at San Bernardino and become a series of faults veining the low-lying Coachella and Imperial valleys, eventually to sink under the waters of the Gulf of California, the blue Sea of Cortez. Why no major earth shifts down south in 1906?

In fact, there had been movement down south that predated the quake of '06. Aerial photographs of the Carrizo Plain revealed just such an action. More than a hundred dry stream-beds intersecting the fault-line at right angles were dramatically offset on the west side twenty to thirty feet north. Any such dislocation had to have been sudden and drastic. Say in the great Fort Tejón quake of 1857, when lateral shifts of twenty to thirty feet were reported. The San Andreas Fault, then, did not move in a single snake-like slither. Rather it did so in segments, one chunk at a time, the western slide always in a northward migration.

Except there were anomalies, contradictions. Some segments did not seem to have suffered any spasms at all. Why? Were they "asleep"? In the middle 1960s, geophysicists closed in on one of these laggard sections—that between Hollister and Cholame, where big quakes are conspicuous by their absence. What they found were buildings seemingly well constructed, slowly being pulled apart at their seams, wooden fences and asphalt pavement that crossed the fault bowing from the northwest to the southeast. Clearly this stretch of the San Andreas did not release its strain in one whopping big crust break, but in an almost imperceptible crawl measured in a few centimeters per year. "Fault creep" described the earth's action between Hollister and Cholame, an action that, all Californians would agree, was infinitely preferable to the "fault lurching" that had shaken San Francisco and the Los Angeles area in the past.

All very intriguing how the 650-mile-long San Andreas Fault behaved differently in different places. Even more curious to the geophysicists trying to piece together the puzzle was the makeup of the earth to the immediate east and west of the fault-line. The two sides did not match. West-side volcanic and sedimentary rock that would complement the east-side rock in age and composition were found as far as 100 miles north, suggesting a long journey of the west side that had taken many millions of years. Furthermore, some east-side rocks were tens of millions of years

A U-2 photo of the San Andreas Fault in one of its most dramatic aspects. The "big split" has formed Tomales Bay in the south (bottom of photo) before angling out to sea around Bodega Head (northern point).

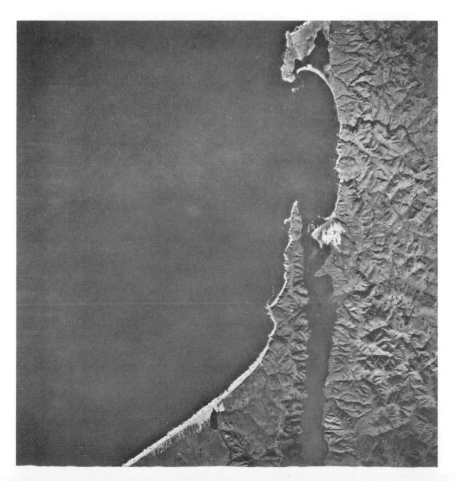

older than the oldest on the Pacific side. It was as though there were two Californias marching in opposite directions and shouldering one another all along the San Andreas Fault.

But why? And what of California's many other faults? Those like the quiescent Garlock, which intersects the San Andreas, or the pesky Hayward that is its parallel east of San Francisco? Or those smaller ones many miles removed, including the Inglewood-Newport and the Mesa, which are alive and active, as has been made perfectly and painfully clear in Long Beach and Santa Barbara? Are all these fractures in the earth's crust somehow interrelated? Do they share the same reasons for being?

The questions invited only cautious speculation. Needed was a conceptual breakthrough. Some sweeping theory of a grand design, whereby the pieces of the puzzle could be assembled to reveal the face of the earth, unmask the mystery of its terrible movements.

Not long after the Americas were discovered and mapped, it was remarked how the coastal configurations of western Africa and eastern South America were complementary, as though the two land masses might have once been joined. In the centuries following, a tentative "piecing together" of North and South America with Europe and Africa continued, supported by similarities in fossil finds in the Old World and the New, as well as by contemporaneous patterns of glaciation. Further conjecture suggested a further contraction of all land masses that went even farther back in time.

The German scientist Alfred E. Wegener formulated the first coherent theory of continental drift, going public with it in a 1912 lecture, but improving upon it in the decades that followed. Trained as an astronomer, then to become a distinguished meteorologist, Wegener, drawing from his wide-ranging observations, had dropped a bombshell on the quiet field of geology. At some time between 135 and 200 million years ago, there was but one continent—Pangaea, he called it. Then, it split in two. Gondwanaland, the southern hemispheric super-continent, subsequently broke up into Africa, South America, Australia, India and other island bits that pepper the southern seas. The northern land bulk, Laurasia, also underwent fracturing, forming Eurasia, North America and Greenland, also to drift and wander separately, likewise intercut by oceans. If one took all these land masses and their shallow continental shelves and fit them together again, they would make Pangaea as it once was.

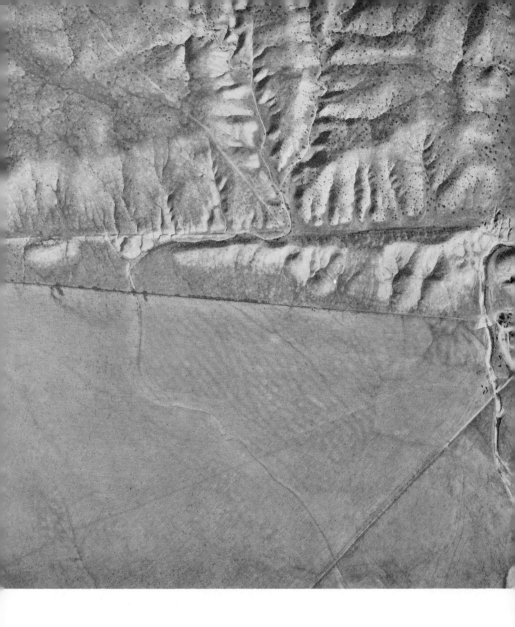

Dramatic evidence that there are "two Californias." Shown here is the central section of the San Andreas Fault, on the Carrizo Plain. Ancient streambeds are dramatically offset where they cross the faultline. The land to the west, which is part of the Pacific Plate, has lurched violently north with respect to interior California, which is part of the westward-moving North American Plate.

Streambeds crossing the faultline on the Carrizo Plain.

Wegener gathered diverse scraps of evidence to support his drifting-of-continents theory. Geodetic surveys early in the century seemed to indicate that Greenland was moving west away from Europe. Fossil beds separated by oceans matched up remarkably when you took away those oceans and closed the land up. And Wegener's specialty, the study of the nature and distribution of ancient climates, was to provide the clincher: beds of glacial boulders and the sands of deserts laid down in geologic time were found in places where glaciation and desert-making simply did not figure if the continents were static; the same for the extensive coal deposits in the northern United States and China, which were a tropical legacy from the Carboniferous Period some 300 million years ago.

Wegener's theory was indeed fascinating, and for a time elicited at least a mixed reaction among earth scientists. But then a slow tide of opposition swelled against the man—a "generalist" untrained in geology—along with his theory which undermined the accepted truths of geology. The earth had evolved from a molten state, was slowly cooling, solidifying from the outside in. In doing so it was contracting, cracking, and creating mountains through the compression of its surface. Crust movement, which could cause earthquakes, was vertical, not horizontal. And those similar fossil finds separated by oceans could be explained by land bridges now sunk beneath the seas.

Wegener countered the latter arguments by invoking the principle of isostasy, which holds that crust surface rock is less dense than what lies below it or under the oceans. How could something light, like a land bridge, "sink" into something heavier?

All the same, the earth Wegener described was too restless and dynamic for the science of his day to accommodate. And his explanation of why Pangaea went to pieces in the first place and the motive force that kept the continents moving (the pull of tides in the earth's crust) was proven absurd by other scientists. Refuted on its weakest point, the whole theory faded into an academic limbo. When Wegener died his followers were few, and his theory of continental drift was widely reviled—particularly in the United States, where generalists are generally looked upon with disfavor.

In the 1950s and 1960s, the science of another day was gathering data that was about as indigestible but far more verifiable than Wegener's ruminations. Seemingly unrelated, or even at odds with some of the fundamental assumptions of modern science, these independent discoveries would merge into a theory that could encompass Wegener's, explain the mechanisms of most earthquakes, and revolutionize the science of geophysics. Global tectonics, or plate tectonics, as it is also called, is still young and immature as grand theories go. But it gives every indication of being here to stay.

The ocean, where life as we know it began, is where plate tectonics was born. On the ocean floor, really, in the 1950s. Shipboard recordings of echoes from explosives detonated on the sea floor showed the earth's crust there surprisingly thin—as little as 3.1 miles in places. This contrasted dramatically with the crust of continents, where the monitoring of seismic waves had indicated an average depth of twenty miles, and up to sixty miles beneath some mountaintops, where mountain roots ran deep. Very interesting, if momentarily baffling.

An even more fascinating discovery at sea in the 1950s was that of sea-bottom rifts bordered with ridges that laced the world's oceans like the seams on a baseball. Minor earthquakes throbbed along these rifts and ridges, suggesting crust activity. As the ships moved away from the ridges, samples of the ocean floor were taken and analyzed. The findings were astonishing, and challenged one of science's oldest, most basic truths: iron particles embedded in those crust samples pointed to magnetic north adjacent to the ridge, as they were supposed to; but farther away, moving out from *both* sides of the ridge, they were found pointing *south!* Moving even farther away, they were oriented north again. Then south again! And so on.

A radical conclusion was in order. The earth's magnetic field periodically did a flip-flop, and if there had been a mariner with a compass some 700,000 years ago, he would have found it pointing south, not north! And by studying the arrangement of those bands of opposite polarity and their widths, one could fix in geologic time when those magnetic reversals took place and draw some heady conclusions about the ridges they paralleled. Along these rises basaltic lava welled up from the earth's upper mantle and cooled off; and the very presence of those parallel bands indicated the sea floor was slowly spreading away from the rift and ridges, leaving a void to be filled by more extrusive matter from the asthenosphere, which cooled and made more crust.

Sea-floor spreading explained those minor quakes along oceanic ridges. Tension was built up as both sides of the sea floor pulled apart, triggering "readjustments" along the earth's crust factories. But then, where did all that crust, in its glacial migration of a few centimeters a year across the floor, go? In the 4.6 billion years the earth has been "living" it would have created an enormous surplus of the light, cool matter on top and lost its balance, its equilibrium. Obviously, the upper mantle was reclaiming its own creation somewhere, somehow.

The ocean floor was found to be scarred by deep trenches as well as ridges, and it is in these depths that scientists believe crust returns to the inner earth. That return is not quiet but attended by earthquakes that may have a deep focus and congregate in mid-oceanic "nests," as in the Tonga Trench, or be more powerful shakes that rise from trenches situated near the meeting place of oceans and continents, as off the coast of South America.

But why does the crust, which is traveling circumferentially around the earth's outer edge, suddenly "take a dive"? What forces are at work to return it to the hot mantle, where it is consumed? That answer among many others is to be found in the bold new theory of plate tectonics.

The world's outer skin, its lithosphere, is composed of a number of separate plates that "float" atop the heavier, hot, viscous asthenosphere. Six is the minimum estimate of the number of such plates, some say there may be as many as twenty, though about a dozen seems to be the present consensus. At any rate, most of these plates are moving slowly. If their directions are divergent, no great harm is done. But if they are on a collision course, they slam, bump and grind against each other, causing earthquakes.

As far as man is concerned, the orneriest of these chunks of wandering lithosphere is the vast Pacific plate, which seems to be in conflict on nearly all its borders. Just how it reacts with another plate seems to depend on where the clash takes place and the thickness of the plates involved. Out in some seismically active oceanic trenches, it apparently dips, slab-like, and at steep angles, under a neighbor plate of about the same thickness, the forces of compression creating earthquakes and thrust-faulting. Off the west coast of South America, the expanding Pacific plate bangs into the smaller Nazca plate, which is pushed against the thick South American plate. The thinner Nazca plate buckles and is forced down and under the South America plate and into the mantle. This subduction zone, as it is called, has been responsible for severe earthquakes and the block-faulting that has long been building the

Looking north from above Los Angeles toward the transverse mountain ranges and, beyond, the San Andreas Fault where it takes a dangerous dogleg direction. The mountains were raised by the compressive forces of two tectonic plates that meet at the San Andreas.

Andes, and more recently "unbuilding" some handsome Spanish colonial cities, with a tragic cost in lives.

To the north and west of the Andean cordillera lies another margin of the Pacific plate and the special case of California. The Golden State, as it turns out, is schizoid, at least geologically. Its southwestern third is the property of the Pacific plate, where ocean ridges long ago created the crust buildup known as the East Pacific Rise. The Pacific plate, and the piece of California that is its passenger, is moving northwest—or trying to. Unfortunately, it is confronted with an obstacle in the massive North American plate that holds title to the remaining two-thirds of California, not to mention the re of North America and a sizeable piece of the Atlantic Ocean behind it. The North American plate has been following Horace Greeley's advice since long before he gave it: it is going west.

The San Andreas Fault is generally accepted as the meeting place of the two plates, where the two irresistible forces confront each other. Something has to give, and that something is California's crust, which has been giving since the North American plate and the East Pacific Rise met between 25 and 30 million years ago.

In one sense, the match is now "even." Along the San Andreas Fault there is no longer any grand-scale over-thrusting or down-dipping or one plate absorbing crust from another. Not just lately. That is ancient prehistory, according to Professor Don L. Anderson of Caltech, an authority on the formation of the San Andreas Fault. Back when the meeting of the plates was young there was subduction taking place, but the North American continent eventually overrode the ridge and choked off the mantle's consumption of local crust. The resultant buildup, the detritus formed by the grinding of the plates, was uplifted to become the southwestern part of California. Even though it has become, politically, a part of North America, it is still attached to the Pacific plate and moves with it in that contrary northwestern direction. And because the contest is now between "equals," the movement along the San Andreas is horizontal, or strike-slip. If the San Andreas were a surgically clean diagonal cut, the two plates might slip by on their separate ways with relative ease, upsetting few orange carts, visiting little grief on the residents of the two Californias. Regretably, the break is jagged, with bends and doglegs dangerously near major population centers—in the San Francisco Bay region

An Air Force U-2 photo looking east toward the great Sierra Nevada (top of photo, under cloud cover) that shows the intersection of the San Andreas and Garlock faults. The former is the big villain in California's seismic history, while the Garlock is now thought to be quiescent.

and the sprawl of Los Angeles. Here, in the areas of impasse, enormous compressive forces are always building, to be spasmodically relieved in earthquakes.

Guessing whether Los Angeles or San Francisco is going to be on the receiving end of the next big San Andreas slip is a game played by many quake watchers, amateur and professional. Often it involves measuring the amount of movement along the fault and deciding which section is lagging and therefore "due." Usually assumed is that the San Andreas is one fault and acts the same in all places, an assumption that does not hold up. Professor Anderson has presented a persuasive case that the northern and southern sections were formed at different geologic times and face different tectonic conditions.

Northern California is earthquake country and Southern California is earthquake country, but they aren't the same country and their seismic problems differ. Along the northern San Andreas, strain is commonly relieved by fault creep. In its southern dogleg near Los Angeles it is not—one reason why a betting person might lay his money down on Los Angeles as the next candidate for a strike-slip nightmare. Another good reason is that the bind near San Francisco was relaxed in 1906, but the strain near Los Angeles has evidently been mounting since 1857.

Over the last twenty-five years Southern California has been more seismically active than Northern California. Strike-slip quakes have been more plentiful down south, below the "locked" link of the San Andreas near the transverse ranges. But a substantial amount of the quake energy expended has also come from vertical movement not directly related to the San Andreas, which marks Southern California as a special case, a seismic smorgasbord, as it were. There the more direct opposition of the North American plate—particularly the deeply anchored batholith known as the San Bernardino Mountains—to the northwestering proclivities of the Pacific plate, is literally making a new geography. Under the exertion of compressive forces, southwestern California is pivoting west, and the boot of Baja California is kicking out into the Pacific, opening wider the Sea of Cortez, causing the rifting and sinking in the Imperial and Coachella valleys. Farther north, near the point of plate contact, where the Pacific plate is trying to shove and vault its way northwest, those same compressive forces are building the transverse ranges, further fracturing the

123

An Air Force U-2 photo of a community built alongside the San Andreas Fault.

earth along such thrust-faults as loosed the Kern County quake of 1952 and the San Fernando quake of 1971.

This tectonic tussle of plates disturbs more than California's major fault. It has created other, secondary faults along lines of crust weakness (all part of the San Andreas system) and is thought by some to be responsible for the broad zone of terrestrial restlessness and deformation that stretches all the way to the Rocky Mountains.

Plate tectonics as a concept is still in its infancy, having only been given a name in 1967. At present it does not explain all earthquakes. Some, such as the great heartland seizure that rocked New Madrid, Missouri, in 1811-12, strike far from any known zones of plate convergence. Why? Some informed guesses are that today's continents are themselves made of previous continental fragments that have merged but are still weak along their former boundaries; that stresses are not confined to the meeting place of plates but are communicated deep into a plate interior; that continents erode and rivers carry heavy loads of particulate matter which are deposited as crust-breaking burdens on certain basins, as in the Mississippi Valley.

Another explanation is wanting. Why do the plates move in the first place? It is thought by some that convective currents from the mantle are responsible. Some suggest that local "hot spots" known to exist around the world, plumes of hot mantle rock that push their way up through the lithosphere, either showing themselves as volcanoes or building subsurface domes, play a part in propelling plates. A divergent if not opposite view is that there is practically no friction between the lithosphere and the slick-topped asthenosphere, so that the plates just slide around, with gravitational attraction as the motive force. Resolving the question of what really moves the plates figures to be the next big breakthrough in plate tectonics.

However imperfectly understood overall, plate tectonics seems right for diagnosing what ails California. Somehow, it seems only fitting that this glamorous, storied meeting place of restless, heterogeneous peoples should also be a meeting place of aimlessly wandering slabs of earth crust. California, as the most vociferous of its boosters will tell you, is "where it's happening," or, if it isn't yet, where it will happen. The same holds true for earthquakes. And for what it is worth, some California-based seismologists aren't too many years away from telling us in advance when a quake will happen, where, and how strong it is likely to be.

12

CALLING
YOUR SHAKES

Californians have reputations for being transcendent sorts. "Crossing over" into mysticism or dabbling in parapsychology or divination comes as naturally as inhaling the balmy Pacific air that rides the prevailing westerly. No surprise then that the subject of earthquakes has long engaged their meditative powers. Few years pass without some seer forecasting disaster for the next April the something-or-other. Usually it is Los Angeles (with San Francisco a close second) that is going to suffer a vengeful shaking, down to its very dust. And it is not uncommon for some true believers to pull up their shallow roots and move on with their cult leaders for cooler, safer, less-sinful climes. But they are the exceptions, not the rule. Most Californians stay put, the date of the next doomsday soon slipping out of mind. They will worry when scientists, not kooks, sound the alarm. If then.

Predicting earthquakes long ranked among the most fragile of man's hopes. As recently as a decade ago, eminent seismologists felt that such a feat was still many generations off, if that great day would ever come. Granted, the Japanese had long observed that a local lifting and subsiding of the land presaged some earthquakes, and the sharp Niigata tremor of 1964 was expected following years of watching the land swell and then sink. But that was almost as helpful as saying, with strong empirical evidence to support you, that Los Angeles or San Francisco would experience a major quake in the next hundred years. A true prediction, if it is to be of much human use, should answer three questions: (1) Where would the quake strike? (2) When would it occur? (3) What would its magnitude be? Failure to hit on all, and within very narrow tolerances, probably would not do the public much good at all. And if the prediction were blown, well then the forecaster would be in as bad shape as the boy who cried wolf.

What seemed a tall, tall order in the sixties has become an imminent possibility in the mid-seventies. In fact, some recent earthquakes have been predicted—their locations pinpointed, their times of occurrence called within the span of a few days, their estimated magnitudes varrying by less than 1.0 from the actual Richter Scale readings. How? What accounted for this happy turnabout in the field of geophysics? For one thing, the theory of plate tectonics brought a previously blurred subject into sharper focus; it gave researchers a big picture to look at and relate their own findings to. This advance was paralleled technologically in the development of sophisticated instruments, including some that were not initially meant for earthquake research, yet found a ready application there.

Ironically, beneficial fallout from the Cold War provided seismologists with some tools they might never have been able to afford. The Department of Defense spent more than $200 million developing seismometers that could detect underground nuclear blasts. Some were more than twenty times more sensitive than those that seismologists already had at their disposal. So when that 8.4 giant quake battered Alaska on Good Friday, 1964, the new instruments scribbled out the story in a depth of detail never before read, and for the first time scientists saw the old glimmer of hope brighten. There was a good chance that earthquakes really could be predicted, and a distinguished panel of scientists recommended that the federal government fund a ten-year prediction program with the price tag of $137 million. But the money was not forthcoming. The Vietnam War was the costly priority item in the 1966 budget.

The disappointment was somewhat softened by the continued borrowings of gadgetry not originally designed for earth science. A tiltmeter meant for navigating spacecraft could be used to measure infinitesimal swellings in the earth. Laser beams flashed across a fault line enabled field surveying teams to make minute measurements of ground movements. Sophisticated computers could be plugged in for rapid analysis of data collected from numerous seismic stations—including some in Baja California powered by solar energy (yet another bequest from space exploration).

From the first, geophysicists knew that prediction depended

upon picking up premonitory signals, slight but noticeable departures from the normal behavior of rocks under stress. These deviations had to be physical, of course, in order to be measured. And the more such precursory anomalies could be found, the better the chances of predicting shakes.

As it turned out, there were several of these anomalies associated with earthquakes. Some, like the surface ooze of oil before the Santa Barbara earthquake of 1925, and the ten-fold increase in oil well casing pressures days before the sharp Kern County temblor of 1952, were known, but of limited usefulness. Not every quake zone has its own oil field. The later discovery of other anomalies in the earth's crust came with the availability of measuring tools, including magnetometers, tiltmeters and strainmeters, and especially the national commitments of quake-plagued China, Japan and the Soviet Union to quake prediction. Japanese scientists observed earth tilts and slumps that preceded earthquakes, as well as sudden changes in local magnetic fields. Russian researchers found a step-up in the electrical conductivity in the affected rock just before the onset of a tremor. They also detected a puzzling increase in the concentrations of the rare radioactive gas radon in Tashkent's well water before that city was slammed by an earthquake in 1966.

There seemed to be no lack of premonitory phenomena. But there was no shortage of questions either, asked more in the U.S. than in the U.S.S.R. or China. Did monitoring really justify the efforts of large field research teams? The expense of measuring devices that could never be deployed in all the world's earthquake zones? How valuable could those seemingly unrelated anomalies really be in giving people accurate advance warnings of quakes in ample time? Finally, was there some principle, some single action in the earth's crust, that might explain them all? Tie them all together?

An almost forgotten clue lay in a laboratory study performed at MIT in the mid-sixties. A team headed by geologist William F. Brace subjected cylindrical-shaped rock samples, similar to what is found in California's crust, to stress tests. Some samples were even sawed in two to simulate faults, then put under great pressure at varying temperatures.

Brace's team learned that the higher the temperatures the more smoothly the rock faces slid past one another, without the strike-slip jerks typical of shallow-focus tremors. Perhaps that ac-

129

counted for California's quakes being confined to the cooler upper crust; at greater depths, approaching the hot mantle, the grating of rock along a fault was "smoothed" out.

The MIT study necessarily had its limitations, as were duly noted. Fault-lines were not smooth, but jagged. Furthermore, small rock samples stressed in a laboratory could not simulate conditions in the earth, where vast chunks of rock of differing makeup are pressured for hundreds of years in unknown ways over mile-upon-mile of fault-line. But the tests produced another result that was worth remembering: When laboratory rock was stressed to about 50 percent of its shattering point, tiny cracks began to open, its electrical conductivity decreased, and seismic waves passing through it were slowed down.

A big break came in 1969 when A.N. Semenov and I.L. Nersevov of Moscow's Institute of Earth Physics, studying earthquakes in the Garm region of Tadzhikistan, discovered a strange thing about that old friend of seismologists everywhere, the P wave. For months before each moderate-size quake, the naturally occurring P waves slowed down, from their normal 1.75 times the speed of the slower S wave, to as little as 1.6 times. Then, just before an earthquake struck, they would return to normal. It seemed to happen every time.

These revelations were shared with American seismologists at a Moscow meeting in 1971, and the visitors could hardly wait to get home and check it out. It seemed to check out, all right, and when related to the work of Brace and others, geophysicists had themselves a hypothesis that might explain those previously observed warning signals, and provide a means to predict many, if not all, earthquakes.

Dilatancy (from the verb dilate, to expand) is the umbrella word for the hypothesis about rock "movements" along faults before an earthquake. Actually dilatancy describes only the first phase of the hypothesis, which has already branched out into two models. In the United States it is mostly dilatancy-diffusion, as proposed by Amos Nur of Stanford University in 1972, and briefly it goes like this: crustal rock subjected to great compressional force, as happens along earthquake faults, expands in volume and tiny cracks appear; water that normally fills the pores in the rock is forced out, much like when you plant your foot on wet beach sand. Air now fills the cracks and pores in the rock, and because the regular P- or pressure-wave velocity depends on the presence of water rather than air, which is less compressible, it slows down as it travels through the dried-out rock. The S or shear wave, meanwhile, remains relatively unaffected and continues at its normal velocity.

There is a point at which the ground water forced out of the expanding rock is forced right back into the cracks and air spaces by surrounding water pressures (the diffusion phase)—again as when water fills the footprint on the sand. With the water back, the P wave reverts to normal. But the returning fluid which momentarily seems to strengthen the already strained rock actually weakens it, and becomes a lubricant for the eventual release of the built-up strain along the fault, in the guise of an earthquake. (In the Russian model, dilatancy-instability, ground water does not play a part; instead there is a rapid increase in cracking, heightened instability and drastic deformation along the fault involved.)

Dilatancy-diffusion could account for the bulging and tilting on the earth's surface prior to a tremor. And water being a better conductor than air, dilatancy-diffusion could explain the rise in electrical conductivity before a quake. Likewise, the increase of the radon isotope in Russian wells could result from more of the expanded rock exposed to water and the greater breakdown of the radioactive mineral washed out of the dilatant zone of rock.

The first successful American prediction based on dilatancy-diffusion was made in the summer of 1973. Graduate student Yash P. Aggarwal at Columbia University's Lamont-Doherty Geological Observatory had his eye on the unstable Blue Mountain Lake area in New York's Adirondacks. In late July seismographs recorded a sudden slowing in P waves, followed shortly by a return to normal. Aggarwal made an excited call to his colleague, Lynn Sykes, at the Lamont-Doherty laboratory. A quake in the 2.5 to 3.0 magnitude range was imminent, he said. Two days later, on August 3, 1973, a 2.5 tremor disturbed the morning calm at Blue Mountain Lake.

Meanwhile, on the other side of the continent, a team of Caltech scientists was scrutinizing the P waves on old records to see if quakes that had already happened couldn't be, as it were, retroactively predicted. James Whitcomb, Jan Garmany, and Don Anderson reported that they could. The records showed a slackening in P-wave speed beginning three-and-a-half years prior to the murderous San Fernando shock of 1971. Some months before it struck, the P waves had, on cue, returned to normal.

131

The Caltech group confirmed other virtues the Russians had found in the P wave behavior. If the velocity fluctuations do occur, there can apparently be only one irreversible result, one release: an earthquake. And where it is going to happen, of course, is roughly where the P waves do their thing. The Caltech team also devised a formula that had an important bearing on the prediction of earthquakes: namely, that the duration of the anomaly is directly related to the magnitude of the quake. That is, the longer the time the P waves slow down, the greater the quake.

The big and open question remaining was: Do the P waves telegraph when a quake will strike? Very likely yes, though few agree on what the rule of thumb should be. Some practitioners say you take between 15 and 25 percent of the total slowdown time and then tack it on the time the P waves revert to normal. That is when you can expect your shake. Others put the waiting time at up to 100 percent; the P waves slow for a year, then go back to normal, and a year later it happens. James Whitcomb, perhaps the most active user of the model, favors a figure more like 50 percent.

The San Fernando quake, and those quakes that had been predicted on the dilatancy model, were all characterized by thrust-faulting, in which earth-shifts are largely vertical and on an angle. What about strike-slip faults, along which the earth moves laterally? California's big, bad one, the San Andreas, is one of those. Could P-wave fluctuations warn of a coming calamity along strike-slip faults?

A team from the University of California, Berkeley, failed to find any seismic signals in their study of records from the side-wheeling central section of the San Andreas. In November of 1973, James Whitcomb of Caltech forecasted a 5.5 quake within three months for the Riverside, California area based on fluctuations in P wave velocity. On January 30, 1974, it rumbled through in advance of deadline, though of a 4.1 magnitude. The type of earth movement could not be determined exactly, but it was not an instance of thrust-faulting.

In the last year or so the initial euphoria over the dilatancy-diffusion hypothesis has died down. The high hopes for it just haven't materialized lately, and even some of its stronger backers now concede that there are some bugs. For one thing, some seismologists feel that the records left on seismograms by the vagrant P waves are just too complicated to read accurately. There are also deep-seated doubts that measured changes in P-wave velocity could ever foretell the occurrence of a truly giant quake, one of those of 8-plus magnitude that have the greatest capacity for mischief; in such a case, the P waves could conceivably go through their slowing-quickening cycle over forty years of time, making their detection a dicey proposition at best. Finally, and most damaging, some earthquakes seem to be preceded by earth behavior that is contrary to what might be expected if dilatancy-diffusion were the explain-all.

Dr. Malcolm Johnston of the U.S.G.S.'s National Center for Earthquake Research in Menlo Park, California, is one who believes the hypothesis has seen better days—though he does not believe that predicting earthquakes is all that far away, either. Johnston played a central role in what might be termed two of modern seismology's great "quiet successes." Back in November of 1974 he was monitoring a network of magnetometers planted near the central San Andreas Fault in the vicinity of Hollister. The instruments at one site recorded a sudden and significant increase in the strength of the local magnetic field before returning to normal. At the same time, tiltmeters six kilometers apart caught the earth in the act of tilting (though not in the direction that could be expected in the dilatancy-diffusion model). It was just the sort of thing one could expect to happen before an earthquake, probably of a magnitude greater than 4.0, Johnston told his colleagues. One associate went further and said that "maybe the earthquake would happen tomorrow."

On the following afternoon, Thanksgiving Day, a 5.2 magnitude tremor briefly rocked Hollister. Records consulted after the fact showed that changes in the velocity of seismic waves also coincided with the changes in ground magnetism and the tilting. Seismologists everywhere had a reason for being thankful.

Geophysicist Johnston was involved in an encore performance on December 30, 1976, after tiltmeters in the Hollister region registered a sudden deformation in the earth along the San Andreas Fault. According to the computations by him and his associates, a 3.5 magnitude earthquake would take place within ten miles of a ranch south of Hollister before a month passed. A week later a 3.2 quakelet thumped the earth within six miles of the ground-zero ranch.

As with the first success, Johnston's "prediction" was strictly for home consumption, being posted on the research facility's bulletin boards. The reason for not giving the forecast a wider circulation was that the quake was only a small one, and there was no reason to alarm the public. Besides, the researchers were calling the shake on what they considered only an experimental model.

Diffusion as an appendage to a hypothesis might not hold much water. Dilatancy may not be all it was cracked up to be. But the P waves apparently remain one of the aspiring quake predictor's best friends. And it was on the basis of the variation of P-wave velocities alone that Caltech's James Whitcomb made public in April of 1976 what was widely interpreted as a prediction of an earthquake for Los Angeles. Although Whitcomb would withdraw his test projection several months later, the initial announcement may yet go down in the story of California and its quakes as a pivotal chapter. At the very least it became the vortex of a gathering storm that has drawn in many individuals and interest groups which are either concerned for California's future or their own, and the two are not necessarily the same.

First, a review of what Whitcomb considered the "testing of a hypothesis," not a prediction. On seismographic recordings, taken north of Los Angeles, of both natural seismic waves and those emanating from quarry blasts, he noticed a slowing of P waves for most of 1974 and 1975. Then, at the end of 1975, they returned to normal. From this data he projected, on the basis of his model, an earthquake of 5.5 to 6.5 magnitude—slightly less than the San Fernando belt of 1971. As to where the quake might occur, he gave as boundaries the town of Fillmore on the west to Mount Baldy on the east, from the Mojave Desert on the north to central Los Angeles on the south. And when? Before April 1, 1977.

Whitcomb's hypothesis was presented before the Governor's Earthquake Council Prediction Advisory Board, a newly formed body of government officials and scientists from public and private institutions charged with the responsibility of screening and evaluating earthquake predictions. The April, 1976 session was open, with the press on hand, and the confab was not, to use one of Howard Cosell's favorite words, halcyon.

Some irresponsible members of the press—from largely outside the Los Angeles area—spread good-bad tidings across the land: an earthquake was predicted for Los Angeles that would humble the proud city of the southern plain. Meanwhile, the Council found fault with Whitcomb's statistical data and couldn't consider it a prediction. At the same time the Council allowed that it wouldn't be surprised if the quake did occur where and when specified. Waffling of a kind, perhaps, but understandable in that semantic thicket where the words "prediction" and "hypothesis" meet.

Whitcomb came out of the hearing unhappy and upset. He resented the "circus atmosphere" of what he considered a public trial. He was, he said, merely presenting a hypothesis for testing, not making a prediction. He had admitted to the Council that he did not have a high level of confidence in the hypothesis; but he still feels—and very strongly—that hypotheses must be publicly aired. Otherwise researchers would trumpet their successes after the fact and bury their mistakes in secret, thereby setting back, perhaps by years, any valid prediction program.

The Whitcomb "prediction" polarized others who were paying attention to what transpired at the Council hearing. On one extreme was the Los Angeles city councilman who threatened to sue Whitcomb, doubtless a gesture calculated to soothe his San Fernando Valley constituents who feared that property values would take a leveling. On the opposite end of the spectrum were the resident paranoids, many of them on the fringes of the physical sciences on Southern California university campuses, who believed that the statement of Whitcomb confirmed their suspicion that geophysicists in the know are "covering up" the facts of an impending cataclysm. Their fears are not easily allayed. (To paraphrase author-critic John Leonard's wry observation, if Watergate taught America's paranoids one thing, it was that they were right all along.)

Between the two extremes stand those who understood what Whitcomb was trying to say and were a bit uneasy, those many who are still in the dark and worry not, and those who understandably confused Whitcomb's "prediction" with another ill omen on the land. The plot was thickening. It even bulged.

The threatening area that Whitcomb has identified happens to overlap strongly what has come to be known in California as the "Palmdale Bulge." This is an ominous swelling centered over the western Mojave Desert that falls partly within Los Angeles' meandering city limits. At least 4,500 square kilometers are involved, and the land has been swelling to a maximum twelve inches for sixteen years, with a spurt in uplift between 1972 and

135

1974. And of as much concern as the vertical rise is a horizontal deformation—a lateral stretching of the desert surface.

Keep in mind that Whitcomb's anomaly was four years old, and the Palmdale uplift is four times that old. The U.S. Geological Survey, which discovered the tumescence just north of the San Gabriel Mountains, has reason to believe the bulge had a part in the San Fernando quake of 1971 and the Point Mugu quake of 1973, and will in thrust-faulting still to come.

But what if it is California's old nemesis acting up again? The San Andreas Fault runs through the swollen area. If it is involved, that could mean, perhaps within a decade, a giant quake on the order of the Fort Tejón shearing of 1857. And that's bad news that the U.S.G.S. has given statistical dimensions to: in Los Angeles and Orange counties alone an estimated 40,000 buildings would collapse or be severely damaged; between 3,000 and 12,000 people would die, with another 12,000 to 48,000 hospitalized; $15 to $25 billion in damage would be done.

If many Southern Californians came down with a case of the anticipatory shakes after word of Whitcomb's "prediction" began to circulate, even more had caught the palsy before the end of November. They were the ones treated to a series of video appearances by one Henry Minturn, a self-professed quake-caller unveiled by Los Angeles television station KNBC as the ultimate weatherman. Minturn prophesied an earthquake for Southern California on or about December 20. Even though the Los Angeles *Times* exposed him as lacking the scientific credentials he claimed, Minturn had his season on the tube, and some impressionable Southern Californians of means made a point of being out of town on doomsday.

Coincidental with the local NBC run of the Henry Minturn show, James Whitcomb withdrew his hypothesis test of a quake by the following spring, relieving at least the secondary symptoms of Southland distress. Then when Minturn's prophecy came up empty at Yuletide and the prophet vanished from the fluid Southern California celebrityscape, there was triple-cause for rejoicing— which also meant forgetting the whole unpleasantness as quickly as possible.

Almost lost under the collective sigh of relief was the reason why Whitcomb has called off his test: the P waves that had slowed and then returned to normal has suddenly and unaccountably slowed again. Not necessarily a good sign at all, though the media-shy Whitcomb declines to publicly speculate on what it all might mean. More unsettling still was the discovery in February of 1977 that the Palmdale Bulge had suddenly sunk in places, with drops of as much as seven inches in a mere three years. Dr. Robert O. Castle, the U.S.G.S. scientist who first identified the swelling a few years back and has been closely monitoring it since, cautions against leaping to any panicky conclusions. No one knows what the ups and downs of the big blister mean. "We are dealing with a unique and surprisingly active region," says Castle, "and we keep coming up with findings that we don't believe or don't know how to assess."

All the same, the late subsidences of the Bulge have prompted the quiet worry of many seismologists. Rapid uplifts and slumps of earth crust have repeatedly prefigured earthquakes, the classic example being the years of surface teetering that climaxed in the battering of Niigata, Japan, in 1964.

So the earthquake danger assumes a new immediacy for Southern Californians, whether they are ready to face it again or not. The frictions and arguments engendered in the spring of 1976 by Whitcomb's "prediction" will be revived, and the overriding question, "What are we going to do about it?", will doubtlessly divide Golden Staters again.

As in most human conflicts, it is not so much a shoot-out between good guys and bad guys, but a competition between the confirmed optimists who try to prepare for the worst and the featherless ostriches who'd rather stick their heads in the adobe of the Promised Land. Among the optimists is California's senior senator Alan Cranston, who has been an advocate of stepped-up earthquake research since 1972, long before the Palmdale Bulge made the papers. For a time the Administration was unresponsive to his urgings of a substantial federal commitment to earthquake prediction. But in 1976, with the flurry of seismic disasters in Guatemala, Italy, China and the Philippines, as well as that worrisome uplift around Palmdale, man's old enemy was at center stage again. Cranston's Earthquake Disaster Mitigation Act breezed through the Senate in May of 1976, and a companion bill seemed headed for clear sailing through the House. Called for was a federal appropriation of $150 million over three years, channeled through the Department of Interior and the National Science Foundation, that would improve land-use planning and quake-resistant structural designs, but primarily to perfect a prediction

137

method that would call a quake two or three days in advance. (The effort, of course, would be concentrated in California, where the seisms and seismologists are.)

Then in September the unexpected happened. The House bill, which called for a somewhat smaller allocation than the Senate version, suffered a stunning defeat, over the protests of the bill's manager Representative George E. Brown and co-sponsor Representative Barry M. Goldwater, Jr. The surprises did not end there, however. Leading the fight against it was Representative William H. Ketchum, whose congressional district includes the Palmdale Bulge! Ketchum called the expenditure a waste of money and went on to say there was no reason to spend millions for something "bureaucrats at the federal level could accomplish with a phone call to the California Division of Mines and Geology." The bald absurdity of that statement has left advocates of an earthquake prediction program pretty much speechless and wondering where they went wrong. The hopes of Cranston and the House sponsors to get the bill reintroduced later in September vaporized when the Ninety-fourth Congress adjourned early before the fall elections.

Many seismologists privately admit the defeat of the legislation was a serious setback to earthquake prediction. That more do not do so loudly and publicly springs from a reluctance that is understandable. Government research grants often come with invisible strings attached . . . here's the money, now solve the problem. Scientific research doesn't work that way. Funds allow scientists to find out whether there is an answer to a problem, not guarantee that answer. That is as true of predicting earthquakes as it is in conquering cancer.

Despite this disappointment, Cranston remains optimistic. He feels that in 1977 the legislation will pass and a comprehensive prediction program will be amply funded. Another optimist is Clarence Allen, professor of geology and geophysics at Caltech and chairman of the National Academy of Science's panel on earthquake prediction. Articulate, by nature a healer, Allen believes that the congressmen who voted the bill down did so out of a misunderstanding of what was at stake, and that with more education and better managing of the legislation by its House sponsors, a large-scale federal commitment to earthquake prediction isn't far off. In the meantime, he is grateful for a release of funds from Washington in 1976, channeled through the U.S.G.S., that has permitted a heavier instrumentation of the Palmdale Bulge area, and while more measurements and measuring devices are sorely needed, Caltech's own effort in operating seismographic stations has more than doubled in the past five years.

Predicting earthquakes is not a plus in everybody's mind. Real estate interests, some engineers and architects, and even a few ivory-tower scientists have long been cool to the idea, for reasons that more often than not are self-serving. They have questioned the wisdom of telling the population of a major urban area that it can expect a slammer within, say, thirty days. What next? Do cities shut down? Court economic death? And where do the threatened people go? And what can they really do to prepare for an impending quake? Why, the panic a prediction could incite would do greater harm than any earthquake!

Admittedly, these arguments are crumbling as reliable quake prediction seems more and more within reach. Moreover, the concerns expressed smell of red herring when the record is consulted. Californians haven't shown any predisposition toward panic in the past even *during* an earthquake. And Whitcomb's and Minturn's "predictions" didn't prompt any grand exodus from Southern California or deflate the high cost of Southland housing.

Sociologist Ralph Turner of UCLA, chairman of the National Academy of Sciences' panel that made a study in 1975 of how earthquake prediction should affect public policy, denounces the whole "panic syndrome" as groundless and ridiculous—and an excuse for public officials to hide from their responsibilities to the people they serve. It isn't panic he fears. It's public indifference to any earthquake warning, aided and abetted by the timidity of public officials.

Perhaps the greatest ally of Americans committed to quake prediction is, superficially, their most unlikely ally: Communist China. In that populous and geologically cursed land, where some geophysicists believe the Indian plate and Pacific plate have the Asian plate in a squeezing vise-grip, seismic tragedy is as old as famine. The Chinese have been the world's greatest losers to earthquakes in the past, and in the present they may very well be its greatest teachers when it comes to predicting them.

Dr. C.B. "Barry" Raleigh of the U.S. Geological Survey, a member of the U.S. seismological delegations that traveled to Red China in the fall of 1974 and again in the summer of 1976 to evaluate Chinese prediction methods, points out that traditionally

139

their great earthquakes have been associated with the fall of dynasties in China, and that the present government has a vested interest in earthquake prediction. This is manifest in 10,000 full-time professional seismologists and another 100,000 trained part-time amateurs at work in China today. No wonder the Chinese speak of the effort as their answer to the Soviet and American space programs.

According to Raleigh, every known quake anomaly is closely monitored . . . P-wave changes, land tilting, local electric and magnetic variations, changes in well-water levels and concentrations of radon, the premonitory actions of animals, the seismic history of an area. But no one anomaly dominates, and it takes the concurrence of several before the Chinese sound a red alert.

Unlike California, where 10 to 20 percent of the structures might fail in a major earthquake, up to 95 percent of the unreinforced masonry buildings in China are hazardous. Therefore the Chinese emphasize short-term prediction, with an eye to saving lives, which are needed for rebuilding cities and rural communes.

Raleigh and others who have visited China are impressed with the results. Prediction, however imperfect (and the Chinese have openly admitted they have made mistakes, and most American seismologists estimate they have batted no higher than .500 in calling the shakes), is thought to be sound in methodology and the program most effective in enlisting the cooperation of the populace.

The most celebrated Chinese success occurred in February of 1975 in Liaoning Province, where every known precursory sign pointed to an earthquake early that month, near the city of Haicheng. On the afternoon of February 4, the Chinese determined the time had come and told the people to quit their homes for the sub-zero winter cold outside. At 7:36 P.M. a 7.3 quake all but leveled Haicheng. Some ten thousand lives had been saved.

The Chinese claim they have predicted more than ten earthquakes of a magnitude greater than 5.0, a claim with which Western seismologists have no inclination to quarrel. It is thought by Raleigh and others who were in the 1976 delegation that the catastrophic July, 1976, 8.2 quake that apparently killed more than 650,000 in and around the industrial city of Tangshan was not predicted. It was not, however, completely unexpected. The Chinese had found indications that a quake would occur there—but it was believed still to be some years off.

Citing a "quake-prediction gap" with China seems a graceless way for Americans to gain support for a national comprehensive program, but it did happen during debate in 1976 in the House of Representatives. Perhaps the ploy will yet ease the passage of federal earthquake mitigation legislation. If and when the additional millions are released for more research and better instrumentation, those who hold the purse strings, and those who live with the fear of earthquakes, will be even more insistent that prediction become a reality. But setting a specific time is not something those working in prediction like doing. While a few earthquakes have been predicted, the art is in no way perfected, and there are still many "ifs" outstanding.

Caltech's Clarence Allen, who thinks quake predicting has been somewhat oversold by the media, does feel that a moderate-size quake will be predicted in the United States within the next five years. As far as prediction becoming anything near routine, he favors something closer to ten years—if all goes well. Ironically, one of the greatest boons to the predictors would be if a sizeable earthquake struck soon, in a well-instrumented area. They are too humane to wish for such a thing; but they do acknowledge that it might teach much of what they still don't know about humankind's age-old scourge.

There is in Senator Cranston's proposed legislation an explicit hope beyond just earthquake prediction. It is earthquake control, or prevention if you can call making harmless little shakes out of big nasty ones prevention. The notion is not as blue-sky as it might seem. Back in the 1960s, the U.S. Army, faced with a major disposal problem at their Rocky Mountain Arsenal, pumped fluid wastes by the hundreds of millions of gallons into a two-mile-deep well over a period of four years. Over that same four years, nearby Denver was jarred by swarms of small quakes. The causal relationship was affirmed in 1966 when the army stopped its waste liquid pumping and Denver got over its case of the jitters just that fast.

U.S. Geological Survey scientists followed up on the Denver experience four years later, in northwest Colorado this time, where Chevron Oil Company was increasing oil recovery by pumping water under pressure into weak-producing wells, and setting off minor seismic events into the bargain. The U.S.G.S., which had been monitoring the miniquakes with seismographs, talked the oil field operators into an experiment. Beginning in October of 1972, water

141

was injected into four Chevron wells and a marked rise in localized tremors was immediate. Come May of 1973, the water was pumped out of the wells and seismic activity abruptly dropped to normal.

Barry Raleigh, who was involved in the experiment, hypothesizes that preventive earthquakes can be manufactured by increasing the fluid pressure on faults, and that control of a near-the-surface, strike-slip fault like the San Andreas may be feasible. The scheme might go like this: wells are dug five kilometers apart and five kilometers deep and the fluid pressure is relieved along the fault; then another well is sunk between the two and water is injected, thus triggering a small quake and releasing the local strain. The fault strain that remains "locked" around the original wells is relieved by the same means as more holes are dug up and down the fault. In this way one makes mini-shakes today of what might build into a monster quake over twenty or thirty years.

The prophets of earthquake prevention have not sent men rushing to their steam shovels yet. The price tag on such a grandiose project would probably run to the billions. And though backers point out, perhaps properly, that a few billions spent in prevention could save many tens of billions in cure, the fat days of federal spending are apparently behind us; austerity budgets have a way of seeing no future beyond next June.

Money aside, and no surprise, schemes for earthquake control have a sizeable number of doubters and detractors. How can one be sure that "quake-priming" will really work? Worse, what if in tinkering with a little one, you inadvertently set off a big one? Maybe an 8-point-plus giant that goes ripping through to a distant major population center? Who will be accountable for the lives lost? Who is legally liable for the possible billions of dollars worth of damage done? Finally, to think the unthinkable, what if a mini-tremor induced in California should trigger a killer quake in China? Japan? Russia? All stand uncertainly on or near the treacherous Pacific Rim, and not enough is known about the possible interrelationships of earthquakes for anyone to go playing tectonic games.

Senator Cranston's legislation makes passing mention of prevention as a future possibility. A small but growing number of scientists are looking into how it can be done. Who knows? Ten years from now earthquake prevention may be the burning issue. Ten years ago some mighty big names were pooh-poohing the whole idea of earthquake prediction.

13

MYTHS AND MAYBES

When the world was flat there was no shortage of explanations for earthquakes. Whatever it was that held up the scheme of things entire, whenever it merely shifted its load, stopped to scratch, or had an understandable muscular spasm, the homeland trembled. Tibetans believed a giant frog carried the earthly table on its back. Some Burmese favored a ring of stalwart snakes as holding the world up. The serviceable water buffalo was both benefactor and occasional terrifier in the East Indies, while in parts of East Africa a great cow was ultimately to blame for those frightening events when it pitched its burden from horn to horn.

The Greeks, born speculators that they were, offered a variety of answers. Poseidon the sea god was responsible for the disturbance in the minds of the religious faithful, because that is where they happened—near the sea. More materialistic thinkers theorized that rainfall or that mysterious "ether" from above seeped into the earth's rock and rendered it unstable. (Those notions cannot be dismissed in their totality even today.)

Ancient peoples, primitive peoples, and primitive ancient peoples alike had the human need to explain natural calamities in the world they knew. Modern science has since swept away many of those fanciful myths, along with the often touching poetry that embroidered them. And yet other myths, perhaps better described as superstition or folklore, survive in the so-called civilized world —even in up-to-date California. And they exist side by side with the new wonderings loosely rooted in science that may or may not yet turn out to be pure science fiction.

One of the most durable myths is largely the making of Hollywood's scarifiers. The celluloid scene is familiar enough, usually signaling the film's climax: The earth trembles, then splits open.

Into the yawning chasm tumble ant-like human forms, some cling-
ing desperately and vainly against the sides of the quaking fissure.
Then the chasm just as dramatically clamps shut, presumably
grinding the hapless victims into fertilizer, but too deep down to
do next year's corn crop any good.

All things are possible of course. It could conceivably happen.
There is even one authenticated case of it really happening, in
Japan in 1948, when a woman field worker is said to have fallen
into a fissure and perished. In California, only livestock have been
reported to have been trapped in earth cracks—in the Owens
Valley in 1872, and along the San Andreas break in 1906. It has
also been reported that in the Fort Tejón quake of 1857 the earth
not only yawned but snapped its mouth closed on some luckless
four-footed critters. One should not waste valuable sack time worrying about a similar fate, however. The odds are about the same
as being brained by a meteorite. Actually, the odds are much
shorter that you will be struck dead by lightning or chomped in
two by a great white shark.

Californians still talk of "earthquake weather," just as they did
more than a century ago when historian James S. Hittel recorded
the prevailing opinion that hot and muggy, still and stagnant air
presaged a shaker. The early Anglo-Californians may well have
adopted this notion from the Hispanos who occupied the tremu-
lous land before them. On the other hand, there is evidence
that the belief that heat and humidity and earthquakes go together is far more widespread, held by peoples oceans apart. The
distinguished Japanese scientist Omori deflated the myth in a
study of eighteen major earthquakes that rocked Japan between
1361 and 1891. In twelve instances he found fair weather heralded
the tremors, on two others it was overcast, raining or snowing on
three, windy and raining on the other. A pretty good cross-section
of Japan's climate. No premonitory pattern whatsoever.

Some old-time Californians remain unconvinced or uninformed.
Often they cite atmospheric conditions just before the Santa
Barbara and Long Beach shocks and they like to remind you that
humidity is a rarity in the Golden State. Well, not as rare as the
boosters of California's climate believe or let on. Memories also
tend to be short and selective. Two of the three giant temblors
that hammered California—the Fort Tejón quake of 1857, and
the Owens Valley quake of 1872—did so when the air was cold
and clear. Historical records, as regretably meager and as sketchy

as they are, fail to support any "earthquake weather" claim; nor do they point to any "earthquake season"—a time of year when the wary ought to be on their guard. Quakes can and do strike without regard to month or weather.

The same sketchy record, however, does at least point to one statistical anomaly. That is the time of day that major quakes have occurred. It has become almost a reflex action for Californians to thank their lucky stars that the feared destroyers have struck at the times when they have, and not at some sidewalk-crowded noon, or when the streets or freeways were filled at 4:30 P.M. And they haven't—even before California had crowded sidewalks or clogged freeways, as the following list of the larger killer quakes will attest:

San Juan Capistrano	1812	8:00 A.M.*
Santa Barbara	1812	10:15 A.M.*
Fort Tejón	1857	8:30 A.M.*
San Francisco	1868	8:00 A.M.*
Owens Valley	1872	2:30 A.M.*
San Francisco	1906	5:12 A.M.
Santa Barbara	1925	6:42 A.M.
Long Beach	1933	5:47 P.M.
Imperial Valley	1940	8:37 P.M.
Kern County	1952	4:52 A.M.
San Fernando	1971	6:01 A.M.

*approximate

With the exception of the evening Long Beach and Imperial County jolts, the dreaded visitations cluster in the early morning hours. Why? Why no noon or mid-afternoon quakes? Coincidence? Or is there a physical explanation? Perhaps the cooling of the earth's crust when the sun is down triggers a release in fault strain through contraction?

Great killer quakes have not been respectors of the busy midday hours elsewhere—not in Tokyo and Yokohama in 1923 when some 100,000 died. Is California's complex geology then somehow different? Or is the sample just too small? If so, will Californians run out of luck next time and make Cassandras of the prophets of doom? That is one unanswered question. There are others.

From far back in time people have reported other natural phenomena concurrent with earthquakes. They claim to have "heard" them, to have observed strange atmospheric lights, to have actually seen the earth's surface roll as though it were an ocean wave. For years scientists tended to dismiss them all as delusions of people in frightened states of mind. Lately, with the continued accumulation of such reports, including some from those trained in the sciences, the skepticism has waned or, as in the case of earthquake sound, vanished altogether.

Since the Alaska shock of 1964, tape recorders that happened to have been going have picked up sounds, often like claps of distant thunder, in a variety of places just as or immediately before the earth began to shake. Chalk it up to serendipity made possible by the age of electronic gadgetry. But as intriguing as the sounds were, the recordings were all made within structures, so that building noises, reverberations, and even human voices all contended. And the earth sounds couldn't be said to have come *directly* from the earth.

During the earthquake swarm that jostled Brawley, California, in January and February of 1975, scientists in the field heard low rumbles from the mini-quakes, and this time an on-the-spot, away-from-civilization experiment was conducted with a combination seismic-acoustic recording unit. A seismometer buried underground and an above-ground microphone both "sensed" three little quakes of 2.8, 2.0 and 2.6 magnitudes in the early morning hours of February 9. The results were affirmative: quakes do create audible sound. David P. Hill of the U.S. Geological Survey team in the field reported its conclusions in the May/June, 1976 issue of the *Earthquake Information Bulletin*. The sound at the recording station arrived at the same time as the Primary waves, and the earth had behaved like an enormous microphone when the P waves reached the ground surface. With low magnitude quakes, according to Hill, P waves are not perceived by humans while the rumbling sounds are. What is felt is the arrival of the more powerful but slower Secondary waves, thus creating the effect of sound traveling in advance of a quake.

Hill speculates that the sounds quakes make are determined largely by the type of rock through which seismic waves travel on their way to the earth surface, the distance from the quake's hypocenter and its magnitude. And in quakes of a magnitude larger than 3, when the fast-moving P waves are strong enough to be felt, the sound of tremor and the shaking will be perceived simultaneously.

The question of atmospheric illumination, variously described as beams or pillars of light and luminous glows in clouds overhead seen even during daylight hours, is more mystifying to scientists—and perhaps may be a crucial and still-puzzling clue to solving the mystery of earthquakes in its entirety. Nineteenth century Californians, among them some learned folks, made much of the lights they said they saw. It led them to believe that earthquakes themselves were somehow electrical in origin.

Later scientists ridiculed the whole idea. The lights were nothing but lightning from a storm that just happened to be occurring at the time—with no causal relationship whatsoever. Or they were caused by a shorting of downed or broken power lines that the bucking earth had snapped. Another explanation was that the mighty earth-wrenching of a quake raised great clouds of dust. Aloft, these swarms of electrically charged particles behaved very much like thunderheads during a storm. Except that would explain illumination *after* an earthquake, not those said to be seen during it.

The stance of scientists has recently retreated from denial to doubt to some cautious acceptance that earthquakes can and do turn on heavenly lights in some as yet unknown way. Again, just too many "reputable" witnesses have seen them. From China come reports that fluorescent lights have gone on during earthquakes when there is no current flowing. In Japan atmospheric lightning has been reliably observed in cloudless skies. Scientists remain steadfast in their opposition to nineteenth century speculation that earthquakes are electrically caused. At the same time they now know that earthquakes are preceded by changes in local electromagnetic patterns within the earth. And the sightings of "quake lights" haven't abated. There is the tantalizing possibility that electrical activity underground, on the earth's surface, right on up to the ionosphere, is somehow interrelated, and that spasms in the earth affect that relationship.

The new open-mindedness now applies to seeing ground waves as well. Dr. Malcolm Johnston of the U.S. Geological Survey's Earthquake Research Center in Menlo Park, California, says it is premature to write off the claim. "It is difficult to understand how they could be seen," he points out, "because the wave-lengths of surface waves are so long that they shouldn't be visible. But so many people have seen them that you simply can't say they're wrong."

CALIFORNIA QUAKE

For every myth demolished in the onward march of modern science there seems to be another article of folk wisdom that survives to challenge scientists or invite them down potentially productive avenues of research. The queer behavior of animals before the onset of a quake is noted over and over in the California record. Dogs yowled, cats complained. Stock became noisy and unruly. It is not just the beasts in the Golden State that acted up, either. Similar reports have been found dating as far back as 700 B.C. and from every seismic quarter. Before the Chilean tremors of 1822 and 1835, sea gulls were said to have made frantic flights inland away from submarine points of imminent rupture. In 1932 a Japanese scientist reported that the normally sluggish catfish became strangely animated before a quake struck. Subsequent reports of Japanese seismologists assert that fishermen in the Sea of Japan have netted seldom-seen deepwater species in the days preceding a suboceanic shock.

This idea that the actions of animals seems to telegraph a terror-to-come has engaged other scientists in the Orient, most particularly in the People's Republic of China. As brand-new and imperfect an art as earthquake prediction is, the long-suffering Chinese, out of necessity, have become its most determined practitioners. No possible precursory sign—P-wave velocity fluctuations, local magnetic changes in the earth, land tilting, raised well water levels, whatever—goes unmonitored. And the observation of animal behavior has an honored place right alongside the other, more mechanical approaches to prediction.

The Chinese, in calling the severe Haicheng tremor of February 4, 1975, say that before the quake rats quit their holes and hibernating snakes slithered up above the ground where they froze to death. Dogs were said to have howled (as they were said to have howled before several past California quakes) and chickens refused to roost at sunset. Since then, Chinese seismologists have kept their eyes and ears open to animal antics right through 1976, a catastrophic year that saw northeast China battered in July by an 8.2 giant quake and a 7.9 aftershock, only to have a 7.2 blow jar central China a few weeks later. The big one in July that destroyed the industrial city of Tangshan and took a heavy toll in human lives apparently was not predicted. But other, lesser tremors were, according to the Chinese, and animal behavior was again a factor in forecasting them. Not only were domesticated animals closely watched, the Peking Zoo menagerie was reported to have put on a noisy and violent show for observers in advance of the tremors.

Precisely why animals seem to act as they do before a quake is not known. Not yet. But speculation flows along two non-contradictory courses. One is that slight earth movements preceding most earthquakes set off subsurface vibrations. These are of a high frequency beyond human sensing. But some animals, especially among the "higher" species—dogs, horses, and the like—do perceive them, react to fears that are instinctual, and sound their alarms.

The other hypothesis applies to more primitive animals, including burrowing beasts and those Chinese snakes who committed suicide. Once more, it relates to those precursory amplitude changes in local electromagnetic fields within the earth. These changes in the creatures' surroundings are interpreted as warnings of coming danger, and man and beast react alike at such times: they flee.

Sino successes in using animals as a kind of earthquake early warning system have not caused much excitement in the American scientific community. The reasons aren't easy to put your finger on, but overall they point to the basic conservatism of that body, which may be both a strength and a failing. As heirs to the English intellectual tradition and the rather valid claims the English can make to being paramount among the founders of modern science, their skepticism leans toward the radical. Animals tipping off humans to imminent quakes smacks of hokum, superstition, metaphysics. Too, Chinese claims are suspect, by some, for political reasons.

Other more receptive American scientists sensibly point out that with seismology teetering on the edge of a brave new age, there are any number of promising paths toward prediction. That American scientists are attracted to the more "mechanical" approaches over studying the behavior of animals should come as no surprise.

All that sounds right and reasonable. But doesn't quite explain away why they are so reluctant to follow up on a promising lead, nor why there are so few animal research projects in motion in the nation. One that is very much in motion is the passion of Ruth Simon, with the U.S. Geological Survey's National Earthquake Information Service in Golden, Colorado. Simon, holding a doctorate in geophysics, and a Ph.D. candidate in biology, is conducting a cross-disciplinary study with an old nuisance of man cast in the role of possible benefactor—the lowly cockroach. Presently she has two colonies of confined roaches being monitored for their life rhythms and behavior. Both reside in California, the odds-on choice for seismic action. One is at Chatsworth, near Los Angeles, and the other is at Anza in the desert northeast of San Diego. Both are situated close to active faults.

Why, of all creatures, cockroaches? Dr. Simon has her reasons, which are all very sound. They are found practically everywhere. They have been around for 250 million years, without undergoing much evolutionary change. They are hardy and can survive in confinement with minimum comforts for long periods of time.

And what does she expect to find? Her caution in answering is true to the scientific method. One isn't supposed to anticipate conclusions, just await and interpret whatever data one gets. But the cockroach program is an outgrowth of Dr. Simon's earlier research on the behavior of cave crickets as influenced by earth tides, which do cause crust deformations that can be recorded on strainmeters. She found that cave crickets became very animated for two or three days before an electrical storm, then "played dead" during the actual storm. Her suspicion is that cockroaches may be sensitive to changes in ground electromagnetism and signal seismic events by departing from their normal rhythms of activity and rest; her preliminary findings, which she is reluctant to discuss just yet, are positive.

Dr. Simon has been conducting her experiment on a now-exhausted shoestring U.S.G.S. grant of $1,700. That it wasn't more, and that other similar projects haven't been funded, clearly suggests that animal behavior as a guide to coming quakes isn't thought a very glamorous line of research. Beyond that looms a spectre that has haunted the physical sciences in America in times past. An unnatural jealousy between disciplines. Specialists are preferred over generalists who would straddle them, even though generalists often conceive new theories that keep specialists gainfully employed for generations.

Some detractors of animal research have questioned how useful the alleged "early warning system" is, and whether it is "early" enough. How long before a quake hits does Fido howl and whine? And is that enough time for you or anyone else to do much getting ready? And how do you know it wasn't an ambulance siren or a stray cat that has upset him? The answers probably won't be in tomorrow's newspaper. All the same, research is just beginning and the quibblers seem unduly hidebound. After all, it seldom takes anyone more than a minute to get out of a building. And most people who get killed in earthquakes are in collapsing buildings. If Fido can give even five minutes' warning of a coming rip, he may be an even greater friend of man than advertised.

It is a long way from the lowly doghouse to the planets of our solar system, but man's quest to know why the earth shakes and, more specifically, to prophesy when it will do so next, has led a few to look far from our terrestrial home for answers. In 1974 two astronomers, John R. Gribbin and Stephen H. Plagemann, published a book entitled *The Jupiter Effect* that ignited controversy in academic circles. The two young men forecast a devastating earthquake for California somewhere along the San Andreas Fault for the early months of 1982. Their reasoning is that in those months all nine planets in the solar system would be in line on one side of the sun, a configuration that occurs only once in every 179 years. The gravitational pull of those heavenly bodies would have little direct effect on the earth. On the sun, however, the planets' combined pull is associated with sun-spot activity and solar flares. Thus, the astronomers' reasoning goes, the resulting step up in solar winds (streams of charged particles) will strike the earth and adversely affect its weather. This in turn will disturb the earth's rotation, slow the spinning globe down, and trigger geologically unstable zones into earthquake action.

Why Gribbin and Plagemann have picked on the San Andreas Fault to the exclusion of others, and marked the Los Angeles area as the favored spot for "one of the greatest disasters of modern times," is not wholly explained by the oft-repeated warning that California's big split is overdue for another big tear. Perhaps the pairing of doom and California, and particularly doom and Los Angeles, is what people want to read. What they will buy.

The Jupiter Effect made few if any converts among earth scientists. Their reaction has ranged from guarded skepticism to dismissal of the whole business as an astrologer's fantasy. William M. Kaula, of UCLA's Department of Planetary and Space Science, wrote one of the most comprehensive critiques for *Science* magazine. He pointed out that there was no flurry of earthquake activity in 1803, the last time the planets were strung out on one side of the sun, faulted the authors for the selectivity of the evidence they cited, and otherwise riddled the thesis with holes. On the basis of the evidence presented, he concluded, there was no reason an earthquake was more likely to occur in 1982 than in 2001, and to say so was like "crying wolf."

Linking earthquakes to the position of our neighbor bodies in the solar system is not new with *The Jupiter Effect,* and it is not just a hobbyhorse of astrologers, either. Since the turn of the century respected scientists have suspected a connection, if for no other than the straightforward physical reason that sun and planets and satellites do exert a gravitational pull on one another. Most recently, Thomas H. Heaton, a graduate student in geophysics at Caltech, conducted a study that limits in time when certain kinds of quakes occur. Heaton concerned himself with the effect the combined gravitational pull of the sun and the moon could have in triggering tremors, and for his investigation he randomly selected 108 earthquakes of magnitudes greater than 5.0 for which the direction of fault movements were known. Thirty-four of the tremors met criteria that lumped them in a class by themselves: they were shallow earthquakes with hypocenters no deeper than thirty kilometers down and each involved vertical earth motions to a significant degree. In all thirty-four cases the quakes occurred when tidal stresses were at or near peak phases, and the odds against it being just coincidence are about 100,000 to one. Heaton concludes that for this particular type of earthquake the tidal forces probably act "as the straw that broke the camel's back, adding just enough additional stress to an already stressed area to trigger the earthquake."

If there is anything to Heaton's study, Californians may have another means of knowing approximately when to get ready, and when to go. That game of hide-and-seek hasn't ever been very popular with them though. Historically, they haven't liked being reminded that the land they build their dreams on is shaky and those dreams could vaporize in a calamitous minute. On the other hand, they may now be ready to face the seismic facts of life, clouded as they are by the myths and the maybes, and decide what they're going to do about them.

14

GETTING READY
FOR THE BIG ONE

Californians do not have the luxury of contemplating what they will do *if* an earthquake strikes. The proper word is *when*. Quakes will come, if not sooner then later. And a giant one will come too, in their lifetimes, or their children's lifetimes, or in their children's children's lifetimes. It is as inevitable as death and increased property taxes.

Given the certainty of earth tremors, Californians would be well-advised to borrow and apply the Boy Scouts' motto and "Be Prepared." In truth, they haven't been very good Scouts in the past. But with earthquake prediction an increasing possibility, maybe fatalism has had its day. Perhaps Californians, bombarded as they are by media messages of a coming disaster at home and the appalling recent losses to quakes abroad, will start getting ready for the next big one.

The late Bailey Willis, the eminent geologist who rode out the Santa Barbara shake of 1925, gave this advice on what to do during an earthquake: "Stand still and count to forty. At the end of that time, it makes no difference what you do." Willis was being only a bit facetious. He knew that panic was a killer quake's greatest ally, and that those who bolted when the earth rocked only increased their chances of winding up on the casualty list. All the same, Willis's advice is downright hazardous to those who happen to be in a bad place when the shaking starts. They're better off to hie themselves elsewhere in a helluva hurry.

Where is the best place to be? Ideally and hypothetically, probably playing centerfield in a fenceless ballpark resting on bedrock in, say, San Diego, the one major California city sufficiently removed from active faults never to have suffered much from recorded earthquakes.

CALIFORNIA QUAKE

Unfortunately, few of us have the legs or skills needed to hold down the centerfield berth, San Diegans have made it perfectly clear they are not interested in urban growth, and besides, if the past is any indicator of the future, the shaking will occur at a time when no games are scheduled. So any preparation scheme must include contingency plans that realistically take into account where you may be and what you might be doing.

Being outdoors and away from any vertical form, man-made or otherwise, is best. California's docile Indians imparted this wisdom to the early Spaniards when, after earthquakes, they abandoned the adobe quarters the padres housed them in and resumed their old lives in flimsy grass and reed shelters. If you are outside when a quake hits, stay as far away as you can from trees, buildings, telephone and power poles and any snapped and crackling electrical lines. The worst that can happen to you is you'll be knocked off your feet. With maybe a few bruises, you'll survive with ineradicable memories of just what power is locked up in the earth that we take for granted.

Of course, few Californians will be lucky enough to be in the open out-of-doors when the quake strikes. That is simply not the way we live. We'll be inside, in our homes, our places of employment, schools, shops, meeting halls, or driving to or from. And it may be in any one of those places that we'll have to see it through.

If you're inside your house or apartment when the shaking starts, move away from the outer walls and any glass windows. Interior halls and bathrooms are usually the safest places to be because the walls have a minimum of ceiling to hold up. If you can't get there, station yourself under the support of a doorway arch, or crouch under a sturdy table or bench. Should the walls actually start tumbling down, assume the fetal position with the hands covering the head. Under no circumstances should you try to run away while a quake is in process.

Home hazards to avoid are hanging mirrors and other heavy wall decorations; tall, spindly furniture with high centers of gravity that are good candidates to fall and break; pieces of furniture that will likely slide when the earth rolls; upright bureaus and bookshelves, which should never be near your bed.

That is the recommended way to survive the actual shaking. Sadly, much grief has come to Californians in the past by what they have done or failed to do *after* the tremor subsided. An immediate inspection should be made of utility outlets. Check for natural gas leaks—with your nose, and not with a candle or cigarette in hand. If you do not smell gas, you're better off to leave things be. Rashly turning off the main gas valve means that you're going to have to relight every single pilot light in your home as soon as you turn it back on. And that means you'd better know exactly how many gas appliances and how many pilot lights you have—and how to light them.

Since water lines are vulnerable to earth shifts, be sure to check your premises for breaks between your residence and the main. If you discover any signs of leakage, shut off the supply at the main valve. Do not drink water that you have any reason to believe may be contaminated. Tap the pantry for its canned soft drinks and juices instead, or just go thirsty until local authorities inform you that the water is potable, which in a big quake, could take a few days.

An all-too-common source of quake damage comes with the upsetting of free-standing hot water heaters—especially those located in the house or garage. If yours is a good candidate for a knockdown, take the precaution of putting in some wood bracing, or even belt or rope it into a secure, upright position.

Electrical conduits can also be broken by a quake. And if the water supply has likewise been affected, a double dose of caution is in order. Inspect electrical appliances. If they are wet, turn off all power at the main circuit box and dry them out before restoring power. The chances are good that any loss of power in your home will originate off your property, at the point of generation or at a relay station. Patience at such times is more than a virtue. Keep your cool and wait. If fuses blow when power is restored, turn off the main switch again and check for short circuits in home wiring and appliances. Remember that if the electricity has been off for some time, food requiring refrigeration may have spoiled. So play it safe; forget for a while the rules of good nutrition, go to the pantry and eat out of cans.

This advice presumes, of course, that your pantry has cans of food to open. But that should be the least preparation of anyone living in earthquake country. Without being either an alarmist or unduly uptight, one is wise to have emergency provisions in the home should something happen. Not just an earthquake, but any major disruption to daily life, man-caused or natural. Designate one place in the home—perhaps an interior closet—as a cache for survival items. Have a pure, sealed water supply there to last, say, five days. Ditto for a few days of ready-to-eat food. Stash some flashlights and extra batteries. Maybe bedding. Certainly a first-aid kit and a transistor radio so you can maintain contact with the outside world whence help, if needed, will eventually come. And familiarize every member of the family with the whereabouts of all utility cut-off switches. Finally, agree on a meeting place should some disaster strike when family members are scattered.

Home is probably the best place to meet, unless it is hard by a quake's epicenter, and even then the chances are it will survive. Particularly if you've done your homework and some preparation. The late Raymond Chandler, in one of his hardboiled novels that pitted private eye Philip Marlowe against the forces of evil and corruption, observed that the wooden front door was the strongest part of the typical California dwelling, the *only* thing one could *not* put a foot or fist through. That may be true, but what is also true is that the same stucco and wooden-frame structure has evolved into one of the best candidates to resist a giant earthquake, providing some basic rules have been adhered to by the builder. Ideally, the house should be bolted to a slab foundation. The floor and the walls should be diagonally braced. Bricks should be sparingly used and bonded by a good cement mortar—as past quakes have tragically demonstrated. From the foundation to the roof, each member should be tied together, with no sparing of nails and cross-bracing, so that the structure moves as a unit when exposed to both vertical and lateral forces.

All other things being equal, a rectangular-shaped building is better, a perfect square probably best. U- or L-shaped structures are not as well endowed to give or flex under the shear stresses that are a specialty of California quakes. And be wary of those architects' dream houses that are beautifully shown in color photographs along with floor plans in Sunday's newspaper supplements. Maybe those tall, steel stilts they rest on are firmly anchored in bedrock; but if you see two stories of glass façade, with or without any vertical means of support, remember that glass has a nasty way of breaking in earthquakes, and flying glass can be lethal.

On the other hand, you can live in the safest house ever built, but if the earth it sits on is faulty, you may still pay a heavy price. Solid bedrock is best. In scientific jargon, ground stability is measured in "coefficients" deviating from the 1.0 base of bedrock. Sedimentary sandstone can vary from a reading of just above 1.0 to more than 2.0, or more than twice the ground shaking of bedrock. With straight sand you multiply by anywhere from two to four times the heave of bedrock. On loose fill multiply by anywhere from four to ten times. And should that fill be water-soaked, you must reckon with a process called "liquefaction." In brief, the super-saturated earth reacts toward a quake's forces as though it were jelly, and large buildings have been known to tilt and sink into the earth as though it were quicksand, which is precisely how that water-filled fill behaves during an earthquake.

The determined survivor will check into the ground his castle rests on. He'll go further and consult maps to see how far he is from active faults—before he buys, if possible. Keep in mind that nowhere are you immune from the threat of earthquake. Do that, and keep in mind that you always improve your survival chances by carefully choosing where you locate.

California has a recent law that aims to curb building on earthquake faults and to let the home buyer know the risks associated with his purchase, and how far from an active fault he is settling. Needless to say, realtors and builders have been cool to the statute, which also requires developers of multiple-family dwellings to study the building sites for surface faulting and fault creep, and that sellers make known to purchasers the hazards they may be buying into. Ignorance and some confusion still surround the administration of the law. But for a nominal fee the wise buyer can purchase detailed maps showing fault zones on more than 250 quadrangles. Eventually, more than 500 zone maps will be available for more than 3,000 miles of active faults in California. In Los Angeles you can buy good fault maps at City Hall, Room 755. In San Francisco, excellent maps reasonably priced can be purchased at the state Division of Mines and Geology office in the Ferry Building.

Knowing the whereabouts of faults is a consideration when buying a home or renting an apartment. Remember, though, that not all faults shown on any map behave the same. When the giant San Andreas moves in those locked sections near Los Angeles and San Francisco, it does so in a big way. The Hayward Fault in Northern California and the Inglewood-Newport and San Jacinto faults in Southern California have deserved reputations as repeat offenders. On the other hand, the sizeable Garlock Fault that cuts across the northern reaches of the Mojave Desert and many lesser faults shown on geologic maps are relatively quiet or asleep, having played their parts in shaping California's surface geography eons ago. Still other faults seem to be awakening. The White

Wolf Fault was a small, unprepossessing "sleeper" before it staggered Kern County with a series of shocks in 1952. More recently, the San Fernando Fault roused itself in February of 1971 after a long period of somnolence and is suspected by seismologists to be capable of causing more trouble in the near future. Fault-finders should keep in mind that bigger active faults are commonly associated with the bigger earthquakes, even though only one segment or section of the fault does the shifting; also, that even small, "sleeping" faults are not the best of neighbors.

Traditionally, Californians have not bought earthquake insurance in any significant numbers. (Standard homeowner policies do not cover quake loss, though they do cover loss due to fire that has been caused by a quake.) But after the San Fernando Valley quake of 1971, the pattern was broken. One Valley agent reported a 500 percent increase in his writing of quake coverage, and though this tapered off in the years following, the April, 1976 "prediction" of a quake by Caltech's James Whitcomb prompted a new surge of buying. Larry Levenson, a Farmers agent, says that among his Valley clients the percentage of those taking out quake insurance has risen from about five to well over thirty.

One reason for this rush to coverage is the inflated real estate market that has prevailed in California the past few years. Middle-income homeowners have suddenly found themselves with $30,000 or $40,000 in equity that begs protecting. That protection isn't exactly cheap. Figure on paying two dollars per thousand dollars of insurance annually. Part of the premium goes toward covering the contents of your home, for which there is a $300 deductible clause. For the structure there is a 5 percent deductible, so if you were insured for $50,000, you would be paying the first $2,500 in repairs out of your own pocket. However steep that may sound, it remains an especially wise investment for those with high equities, for earthquake claims tend to be hefty.

Deciding on earthquake insurance is one thing. Securing it is quite another. Four of the larger companies, including Safeco, will not write it. Other companies will write it but they don't push it. If you want it, you'll probably have to go to your agent rather than vice versa. Farmers, State Farm, and Hartford are among the big firms still offering earthquake coverage. But how long they or other companies will continue to service existing insureds or write new policies is unclear. A Department of Interior study foresees the impossibility of private companies covering claims of between

$10 billion and $25 billion, the range of potential loss that can be expected from a giant quake striking near a major urban area. Should the private companies cease writing insurance and the state or federal governments do not fill the void in some way, home-owners could find themselves in a terrible squeeze. Some mortgage lenders—though still relatively few—already require earthquake insurance in higher risk areas.

Coming through a big quake at home with your house reasonably intact and your property protected is something you can attend to. But if you're away from home when it hits, you face a different set of circumstances. One is more dependent on plans made or unmade by others. What to do is less clear, chances of survival are more dicey.

Perhaps as good a place to be as any when the distinctive rumble is heard is in your car. Yes, a few motorists have lost their lives during tremors, in the Long Beach quake and those since. But they are very few, and despite the enormous increase in auto-mobiles on California's roads at any given time now, an early recognition of what is happening and the exercise of plain common sense should see you safely through. If you're behind the wheel when a quake hits, make your way to the right side of the road, as safety permits. Stop and then stay put. Your car may bounce on its springs like a seismometer, but you've got a turtle's shell of pro-tection around you that you'd be foolish to shed. Once the tremor spends itself, you're best off to head for home, being especially watchful for road hazards the quake may have caused. Once at your haven, stay put. Emergency vehicles will doubtlessly be on the streets heading for stricken areas. Resist the urge to follow. There'll always be time to sightsee for weeks afterwards, when you will not impede rescue operations.

Of all possible road hazards, be most alert to downed bridges and freeway overpasses. Since the 1971 quake, when soaring rib-bons of steel and concrete came down in pieces atop Interstate 5, the Division of Highways has upgraded the design of overpasses, and in mid-1976 more than $12 million was allocated to make 630 freeway structures earthquake-resistant. How resistant? The San Fernando quake was a moderate tremor. A severe or giant quake might not be resistable.

California's school children are not the defenseless hostages to seismic fortune they once were. Following the near disaster in Long Beach in 1933, the state established an upgraded code for all schools. But the question remains, will the new classrooms stand up in a really big one? The answer is contained in at least two questions that pertain to all structures that Californians build: How big is that big one? And how close to the destructive waves unleashed is the structure? It is a reassuring sign of the times that for three million California school children earthquake drills have lately taken their rightful place alongside fire drills. There is an important difference in procedure, however. Instead of an orderly filing out of the building, pupils are taught to crawl under their desks and assume the tuck position.

Many an adult Californian spends forty or more hours a week in one of the clean, functional, air-conditioned towers that have been popping up like long-stemmed mushrooms from the Golden State's cities these past twenty years. The skyscraper is the twentieth century's answer to Chartres, the Parthenon, and the pyramids. And Californians are no less enamored of these visible symbols of prestige and power than cosmopolites elsewhere. Probably, as relative newcomers generally on the make, they're a little more so. The upshot has been the repeal of old statutory limits on building height and the new rise of urban high-rise; and more quake questions: How high? How safe?

Some very reputable architects and engineers have staked their reputations on the safety of the towers. They say that a well-designed steel-reinforced tall building will sway and not break, and be standing when virtually all other structures are rubble. They have their critics, many of them academics not involved in the actual building. Some have reservations not about the basic structure standing, but about what is going to happen to the "skins" and "fins," the ornamental façades and the over-use of un-cushioned glass, when they come unglued. Those inside may come through it all in fine shape. But what about those down below, on the street?

Other skeptics challenge the actual standing power of the high-risers if they were tested by a Maximum Credible Earthquake (MCE), which in Los Angeles and San Francisco is thought to be about 8.5 on the Richter Scale, if the San Andreas were involved. Moreover, they are deeply concerned with quakes of lesser magnitudes that have especially destructive properties. Surface waves tend to travel at different speeds; the tall towers are built to bend, and have their own natural periods of sway. The danger is that a train of long-period surface waves might be harmonious with the natural period of the building and shake it beyond any designer's imagining.

The high-rise trial continues, with both sides believing they are right. Right now the jury is out. Both sides would agree that the best thing would be for it to remain out, permanently.

There are buildings in California that aren't homes, schools, or high-rises, in which one should definitely not be during an earthquake: they are estimated to number as many as 100,000, and are the older structures of unreinforced masonry, brick or hollow tile walls that went up before building codes were tightened in the 1930s. According to Karl V. Steinbrugge, professor of structural design at the University of California, Berkeley, and chairman of the state's Seismic Safety Commission, they differ not at all from the buildings which collapsed in China in July of 1976 and killed over 650,000.

What especially worries Steinbrugge and others is the usage patterns of these buildings. A disproportionately high number of them are crowd drawers—churches, auditoriums, theaters, and meeting halls. In quakes past, in California and elsewhere, the lesson has been there for the learning: loss of life is not evenly distributed over the shaken area, but clusters precisely where these substandard buildings stand and then fall.

In Los Angeles, some 14,000 such candidates for a razing have been identified; in San Francisco they counted up to 900 and then quit when a lot of people got upset. Who does the razing—man with forethought or nature with its familiar fury—is an open question. The smart money, however, favors nature and disaster. The cost of replacing the structures is prohibitive, and the estimates for bringing the buildings up to code strength in these inflationary times runs as high as 80 percent of replacement costs.

In 1976, Assemblyman Paul Carpenter of Garden Grove submitted a bill to the state legislature requiring that all such structures be signed, identifying them as hazardous places to be during an earthquake. The bill died in committee under real estate pressure. The City of Los Angeles passed its own labeling ordinance, but a concerned Los Angeles *Times* questions its adequacy. Identifying structures as dangerous places to be during a severe earthquake may be a step in the right direction, but it is a mincing step at best and not without its aspect of macabre humor. Recently

161

the Los Angeles City Council's Building and Safety Committee recommended to the full Council that all unreinforced masonry buildings be strengthened to code over the next ten years. If this is not done, then the structures should be vacated. The *Times* agrees, and puts at least part of the financial responsibility, which could amount to $5 billion, back on the shoulders of the federal government. Money is not now available for making buildings safe, the *Times* observes. But when the worst does come, the federal government can be expected to offer even more billions in after-the-fact dollar aid.

For the present, Californians will continue to assemble in their houses of worship, go to club meetings, and fill ornate old theaters for an evening's entertainment. They will continue to do so with a certain degree of risk. Perhaps the temblors will serve their own warnings. Some do, of course, in slight foreshocks that presage more violent slides along a fault line. But these can not be sorted from the many minor tremors that rattle dishes and set overhead lights to swinging throughout California every year. To make mat-ters worse, some major quakes strike without any discernible foreshocks at all.

Aftershocks are far more predictable. In moderate to giant quakes they are all but inevitable. So if your church or club or place of employment is damaged in a quake but not destroyed, you might stay away awhile. Chances are, though, that there will already be signs, newly posted, advising you to do that very thing.

California's crust is seamed with hundreds of faults. On maps they resemble a lot of dozing snakes generally nesting closer to major population centers than in the boondocks. Which ones will wiggle next, and when, are a worry not only to homeowners, high-rise workers, and socializers, but to those who construct the massive public projects that serve the state's population centers.

Water is the vital life fluid, and in California it has always been in short supply. Historically, men have repeatedly cheated, stolen and even killed to get their share of it—and often more than their fair share. In the 1960s the state went forward with its massive California Water Project and brought some semblance of order, if not harmony, to the competition. In one of the most ambitious of human undertakings, water-surplus areas north of San Francisco were tapped by a more than 400-mile-long network of canals, aqueducts, tunnels, conduits, reservoirs, and pumping stations to slake the thirst of the populous south. And that multi-branched system has run head-on into one or more of California's biggest sleeping snakes at practically every turn.

The westward-reaching branch that delivers water to the Bay Area south of San Francisco must contend with the Hayward Fault. The arm that will extend west to the coast communities of Central California must cross the San Andreas. The most important artery, the one that carries the life fluid to parched Southern California, encounters the Garlock Fault and crosses the San Andreas four separate times.

The California Department of Water Resources has tred warily over these serpents. Conceding the virtual impossibility of building lines that would resist shocks the size of those in 1857 and 1906, its strategy is consciously defensive. Wherever possible, surface canals have replaced the cheaper-to-build but more inaccessible tunnels at points where active faults, mountains and water-flow meet. Quick access and rapid repair will be the tactical responses, and to this end roads capable of carrying heavy equipment have been cut at the danger points. At probably the most dangerous point of all, where the Tehachapi Mountains and the San Andreas share space, several automatic gates have been installed to stop the southward flow of water should the worst happen.

If California's water system has a weak link, its dammed reservoirs are the primary suspects. The near-miss with disaster at the Van Norman Lakes in February of 1971 is fresh in many minds. Fresher still is the tragic collapse of the Teton Dam in early June of 1976. Seismic activity was not responsible for the torrential release of 80 billion gallons of water on the Upper Snake that killed eleven Idahoans and did about $1.5 billion in property damage; human error within the Bureau of Reclamation was.

But both incidents have contributed to a controversy that recently peaked in Northern California, where the Bureau of Reclamation intends to build a much larger dam in a seismically active area. As designed, Auburn Dam on the North Fork of the American River would be a thin, double-curvature, high-arch barrier 685 feet high and 4,150 feet wide at its crest, the first of its kind in California, and the largest of its kind in the world.

Bureau of Reclamation engineers have maintained that the dam will stand up to the maximum earthquake the region can expect, suffering no more than cracks that can be repaired. Other engineers have hotly disputed the claim and the design. What has fueled the controversy is a surprise quake that struck Butte County on August 1, 1975, in the vicinity of the Oroville Dam on the Feather River. That mammoth earthen barrier, built by the State of California, came through the sizeable shake in good shape. But it also drew attention to the seismicity of the region and the possible presence of other unknown faults in the foothills of the Sierra Nevada. Furthermore, it lends support to those who claim, with strong scientific evidence on their side, that the actual impounding of waters which seep deep into the earth's crust causes earthquakes.

The Bureau of Reclamation has bowed to pressure and hired a private, outside consulting firm and assembled a board of consultants to review their design for possible modifications. But it still wants to begin construction this year. Senator Alan Cranston, though a backer of the Auburn Dam, favors a halt to the project until the points of controversy have been resolved by further studies. He tried to get the first $18 million deleted from the 1977 budget, and though he failed, construction has been delayed for other reasons, and the big worry is temporarily on the shelf. That worry? That a quake would cause Auburn Dam to fail and send a 100-foot-high wall of water rushing down the American River gorge, topping the Folsom and Natomas dams, to wash away the city of Sacramento.

In June of 1976, Californians were presented with a ballot initiative that meant to slow drastically the development of nuclear power in the state. On an issue that drew nationwide attention, Californians voted decisively against the initiative and for nuclear power as a future energy source. The issue was bitterly contested, despite the lopsided ballot count, and opponents of nuclear facilities made much of the seismic risks involved . . . what would happen if a tremor ravaged a plant and released radioactive matter into the environment?

The naysayers were not without grounds for their concern. In the past, nuclear plants, both in the planning and building stages, had to be aborted due to the threat of possible earthquakes. Pacific Gas and Electric began work on its Bodega Bay nuclear facility in the early 1960s, but after the expenditure of millions of dollars, a discontinuity in the rock was discovered at the excavation site, which was only two miles west of the San Andreas. At the time there were no federal regulations dealing with the fault location problem and the Bodega Bay site was abandoned. As the Code of Federal Regulations governing the design of nuclear plants was being amended, plans were drawn for a nuclear facility at Malibu in Southern California. It too was scuttled when it failed to meet the newly drafted regulations governing seismicity. Then a third plant, slated for Mendocino, was aborted because of the expense of building it to withstand the maximum forces which a quake could unleash locally.

The experiences of the sixties pointed to a knowledge gap between the know-how to build nuclear plants and what geologists were still learning about newly discovered faults and the interrelationship of those already identified. That gap is narrowing, but the repercussions of past actions are still with us. A case in point is PG&E's twin Diablo Canyon nuclear installations near San Luis Obispo. When designed a decade ago, they were thought by all to be well above specifications. But then geologists found that an offshore chain of faults were probably interrelated and therefore capable of producing an earthquake of a magnitude not previously conceived possible. Now the Diablo Canyon plants, one of which was scheduled to become operational in 1976, are in limbo.

A structure's strength is generally measured in terms of the horizontal ground acceleration, or "G" force, that it can flex to without breaking. One G equals the acceleration of gravity, or 32 feet per second, and a building's percentage of overall strength is determined in large part by the quantity and quality of the concrete and steel that are used in construction.

The Diablo Canyon plants have been built to withstand an 0.4 G loading, but the Nuclear Regulatory Commission is now requiring PG&E to go to 0.75 G of sustained acceleration. (Sustained acceleration is a new concept that replaces the old yardstick of peak acceleration, the rationale being that a structure should be able to hold up under sustained shaking.) As the matter now stands, the first of the Diablo Canyon plants probably won't go "critical" for another year.

California's power companies and the Nuclear Regulatory Commission are now approaching the quake danger with a greater awareness and respect, concerned not only with plants to be built, but those already in operation. The NRC issues provisional operating permits which must be renewed periodically, and it is at these times that the federal agency can require structural upgrading to what it deems necessary to resist the forces of the worst possible

165

accident inside and the biggest possible earthquake outside *at the same time*.

At present, California's oldest nuclear power station, at Humboldt Bay near Eureka, is being strengthened from 0.25 G to 0.50 G. And on the Southern California coast the operational unit at San Onofre is being upgraded from 0.50 to 0.67 G, to match the two companion units under construction.

There is general agreement now that California's nuclear power plants are the strongest structures ever built by man and will remain safely intact after everything else is knocked flat. Edward Keith, executive vice president of EDS Nuclear, believes that is certain, and as a consultant in earthquake engineering he has been in on several other projects, including the high-rise Bank of America building in San Francisco and the Alaska pipeline. Keith finds many more valid worries than the failure of a nuclear power station. His pet concerns are the underground utility systems and most particularly the sewage systems that have been neglected entirely. No rule, code, regulation, or law exists to make them seismically resistant, and the segmented pipe used in them is a prime candidate to break during a quake and pose a health hazard that no one has yet been willing to face.

How prepared California will be to meet its next big quake is largely a matter of timing: when the earth chooses to move and what humans choose to do between now and then. Prevention is still measured in ounces, cure in pounds. Unfortunately, more people in positions of responsibility have lately been thinking pounds-later rather than ounces-now. Last year Assemblyman Carpenter authored three separate bills dealing with earthquake mitigation; all died of the fiscal chill in Sacramento. This year Carpenter, now a state senator, has introduced S.B. 135, which would establish a California Earthquake Prediction System and staff a Prediction Analysis Center answerable to the State Geologist. More than $16 million are being requested over the next three years to train and maintain the body of technicians who would be responsible for predicting earthquakes, and there are doubts aplenty that the state's lawmakers will find the funds for so ambitious a plan.

There are some hopeful signs: scientists are closing in on the old dream of prediction, and public awareness of the danger is at an

166

all-time high; the state recently passed a law requiring hospitals to be built to the same code requirements as high-rise buildings. And the state Office of Emergency Services has recruited Bugs Bunny and Daffy Duck for TV spots that tell citizens what to do before, during, and after a quake.

But there is much more to be done, and most assuredly it cannot all be done by Californians. Federal action must follow any major California quake because only the federal government has the resources to meet the magnitude of expected loss. Besides, the nation cannot afford a crippled California, for pragmatic as well as humanitarian reasons. It would be nice if some of that assistance arrived before the quake, but it shouldn't be counted on.

Californians in the meantime will stand their unsteady ground in sybaritic ignorance or in some state of worried preparation for the next spasm in the Promised Land. Most of the worrywarts might console themselves with a slogan coined here: At Least I Don't Live in Daly City. In that Peninsula community, some folks have built houses right over the San Andreas Fault that ripped apart in 1906, and other folks in their finite wisdom have since called them home. As for those who live in Daly City, well, life has to have some risks to be interesting. All that sunshine and good life don't come for free.

INDEX

169